The Traumatic Past and Uncertain Future of South Sudan

Perspective from Social Responsibility on Local and Global issues
& the relentless struggle for education.

———

NHIAL THIWAT RUACH

authorHOUSE®

AuthorHouse™
1663 Liberty Drive
Bloomington, IN 47403
www.authorhouse.com
Phone: 1 (800) 839-8640

Published by AuthorHouse   10/13/2015

ISBN: 978-1-5049-5394-8 (sc)
ISBN: 978-1-5049-5393-1 (e)

Print information available on the last page.

CONTENTS

ACKNOWLEDGEMENTS

First and foremost, I give many thanks to the Almighty for guaranteeing my health and my safety in many years of travelling from a country to another in search of education and for giving me the courage that has kept me away from destructive life styles that could have easily derailed my educational pursuit as I have lived apart from my parents ever since at the age of twelve. Without values instilled in me by my parents as well as by the Gospel, I could be a different person today and I would probably not have an ambition to achieve my education. I also give much gratitude to my father (Thiwat Ruach MongJiek) and my late mother (Nyakuon Riak Ayuel) for their tremendous faith in me by allowing me to pursue my education in foreign countries at a very young age. I am grateful to them for valuing the education and allowed me to pursue this goal far from them and alone with no parental guidance. Many thanks to my late uncle (Gatluak Ruach Mongjiek) who also inspired me through education.

I extend my appreciation to Mr. Simon Lul Chamyang and others who taught me how to read and write in my native language, Thok Naath (Nuer Language) which later inspired me to learn the English language. I also extend my appreciation to Mr. Gang Lual Banyker and his family for their generosity and for allowing me to stay with them while attending Gambella Secondary School in Ethiopia. I also give tremendous recognition to my Master program's coordinator and academic advisor Dr. Julie Andrzejewski for accepting me into the Social Responsibility program and for her inspiration that led me to expand my interest in Social justice, Peace, Environmental Justice, and Animal justice. Thank to Mr. Garry Byron, my Academic advisor and Electronic Engineering coordinator at South Dakota State University. Last but not least, I give many thanks to my Master's programs committee; Dr. Julie Andzejewski, Dr. John Alessio, Dr. Mwangi Mumbi for their guidance and their unwavering faith in me. I give much gratitude to everyone else that has directly or indirectly contributed in my educational success starting from my village in South Sudan and continue on here in USA. Without their contributions my educational ambition would not have been possible.

INTRODUCTION

This book is focused on the country of South Sudan with the intention to alert its leaders and citizens about the evils of neoliberalism. Meanwhile South Sudan is a young nation that has just emerged from many decades of civil war. So far it has not been directly affected by corporations and neoliberal policies, expressing such concern will give South Sudan leaders an opportunity to put in place a political and economic policies that are geared towards development; socially, politically, and economically in the youngest nation. Accordingly, leaders of this newly formed country need to be informed about corporate destruction, done in the name of progress, so that they are conscious of consequential threats. Additionally, this book examines post-colonial and post-independence challenges facing the country as it transitions into becoming a nation state. Other focuses will be on external and internal factors that hinder the implementation of good governance, delivery of services to the people, preservation of the environment and natural resources, and the unity among South Sudan's multiple ethnicities. While positioning myself as South Sudanese, I briefly touch on my personal journey in pursuit of elementary and higher education, a lengthy and a rough journey that began in my country that has been ravaged by a civil war. In addition, the analysis of issues is drawn from theoretical work of Marx, Fanon, Parenti, and many others who advance the need for critical understanding of global unequal power relation

Furthermore, one of the reasons I am compelled to write this book on the South Sudan is my firm affection for the people of South Sudan. Despite the fact that I grew up in different countries and have been away from South Sudan for more than two decades, nevertheless, I remain connected by birth and share the grief with the South Sudanese people. Given that my parents, siblings, and relatives lived in South Sudan throughout the war and endured a lot of sufferings, it would be devastating to see them undergo additional sufferings being imposed on them by the foreign governments, corporations, and corrupt government officials who may only pursue their personal interests at the expense of the general population within the country.

Hence, having studied global politics in the Social Responsibility program, I am dreadfully concerned that foreign governments will meddle in South Sudan politic as they have done it in global context. Therefore, concerned leaders in South Sudan ought to to be vigilant on the subject of external influences from foreign countries, institutions, and corporations whose purpose is only to carry out neo-imperialistic visions through neoliberal policies. If not heeded, the imperialism will once again reveal itself in South Sudan as it did to other African countries during the colonial period. As Parenti points out that, "Cooperative lands are supplanted by agribusiness factory farms, villages by desolate shanty towns, autonomous regions by centralized autocracies" (1995). So, South Sudan has an opportunity to resist those destructions which many developing countries have experienced from corporatocracies. For all those reasons, I am obliged to write and expose potential problems that will cause destruction and misery in this new nation.

BRIEF HISTORY OF THE SUDANESE CONFLICT

Issues such as social justice, peace and war, the environment, and treatment of all forms of life are interconnected. When there is an absence of social justice in any society it affects peace. When citizens are oppressed and inequality exists in any society, it leads to discrimination and marginalization based on race/tribe, origin, or sexual orientation. As a result, the rights of certain groups or people are denied which leads to poverty due to lack of opportunities or blocked opportunities for those experiencing prejudice. Thus, people begin to build hatred toward each other which leads to social uprisings or social movements and ultimately leads to war. Consequently, innocent people become victims and lose their lives; some become homeless and force to migrate to different regions or countries. This had been a case in Sudan during the civil war.

The Sudan civil war is believed to be one of the most savage and the longest conflicts in the continent of Africa. "This war has raged intermittently since 1955, making it possibly the longest conflict in the world" (*New African,* 2012). This war broke out between African-Christian South and Arab-Muslim North over many issues such as domination and continued after the country gained its independence from the British. As stated on the Sudan People Liberation Army (SPLA) website, *http:// www.splmtoday.com,* "The failure of the colonial authorities to allow the people of what British Empire used to call 'Closed Districts' (South Sudan, Nuba Mountain, Darfur, and Blue Nile) to exercise their right to self-determination became one of the main factors that contributed to the first civil war in Sudan from 1955-1972" (*SPLA Today,* 2007). Whereas, "Marginalization in all its forms, discrimination, injustice and subordination, constituted the root causes of the conflict" *(New African,* 2012).

In 1930s, the British declared South Sudan to be culturally and racially distinct from the North. The Empire suggested that the South would need to be developed as a separate territory from the North and integrated it into the British-East African colonies. So, African culture and language as well as Christianity thrived in the South with the elimination of Arab or Islamic connections. While North Sudan was added to British-North-Africa colonies, and its cultural orientation was toward Islamic and Arab. As explained in *Middle East Quarterly*,

> The North, with roughly two-thirds of Sudan's land and population, is Muslim and Arabic-speaking; the Northern identity is an inseparable amalgamation of Islam and the Arabic language. The South is more indigenously African in race, culture, and religion; its identity is indigenously African, with Christian influences and a Western orientation. (Deng, 2001)

The separate imperial government system established by the British in the former Sudan had temporarily eliminated Arab and Moslem influence in the South Sudan throughout the 1940s. However, the British Empire had a change of heart regarding this separate imperial government system and its policy after numerous disputes and resistances from indigenous in the South during the attempt to conquer their region. As a result, the British Empire decided to hand over the country to the Arab-North during independence to revenge and to punish the indigenous people in the South. Consequently, people of South Sudan generally felt that what happened at independence was a mere substitution of one set of colonial masters for another which they predicted that the upcoming master would be a worst type. Therefore, this division and superiority (social stratification) set up by the British Empire in Sudan allowed people of Arab descent in the North to dominate political and economic power over the peoples of African-descent in the South, Nuba Mountain, Darfur, and Blue Nile. As stated,

> The root causes of the conflict in Sudan are a combination of the institutional legacy of colonialism, and deliberate policies by each postcolonial government to marginalize socially, politically and economically peripheral regions. Socio-economic disparity and structural inequalities have been the product of the colonial and postcolonial policy. (*New African, 2012*)

This spatial injustice became obvious in the formation of government when South and other regions were underrepresented in the central Government. While majority of resources were concentrated in the North.

"Underdevelopment was [sic] characterizing most of the Sudan outside of the Central Region, the most of colonial and post-colonial investment. This pattern of unequal development continued after independence because the majority of post-independence government, it was claimed that, it had been in the hands of mostly people from developed areas" (Johnson, 2003).

THE BEGINNING OF THE FIRST CIVIL WAR AND FORMATION OF THE MOVEMENTS

When Sudan gained its independence from British in 1956, there was rebellion already under way in the South due to apprehension of marginalization and others issues.

Southern Sudanese, black and overwhelmingly non-Muslim, feared that national independence simply meant a replacement of British imperial rule by Northern Sudanese Arab colonialism. Indeed, their fears were well founded, as Southerners suffered discriminations and abuses from Northern governments seeking to create a Muslim and Arabized country. (*The Nation, 2007*)

The disproportionate representation and unfair allocation of resources and services existed beyond imagination in the South. Johnson states, "Unequal distribution of educational facilities throughout the South and the uneven incorporation of educated persons within structure of Native Administrations were largely the results of administrative decisions taken by British officials either in Khartoum or in the provinces" (2003).

Thus, Southerners resented those policies and reacted by protesting in many towns in the South. On August 18, 1955, Southern units of the Sudan Defense Force stationed in the Southern town of Torit revolted. This revolt took place four months before Sudan declared its independence upon learning the impending independence of the Sudan as one country under Northern domination. After learning of the rebellion, government troops were flown in from their garrisons in the North to quell revolt in the Southern regions and ended up committing atrocities against civilians by killing, looting, and burning several villages as a punishment for sheltering mutineers.

"The army began to burn villages in late 1950s. Such repressive activities, especially those aimed at educated southern Sudanese, increased opposition to the government. This was met by further repressive action, including arrest and torture of civilians" (Johnson, 2003).

Consequently, the African-Christians in the South grew more anti-Muslim and Arab. This resentment led to widely supported rebellion by the people of the South. As a result, "A number of senior political figures (including Fr. Santurnino Lohure, Aggrey Jaden, Joseph Oduho, and William Deng) as well as a far greater number of students, left for the bush and neighboring countries where they joined with the remaining mutineers to form both an exile political movement and the core of a guerrilla army" (Johnson, 2003). In 1963, two years after the rebellion in the South, the first rebel movement known as Southern Sudan Liberation Movement (SSLM) and its military wing the "Anya-nya" guerrilla army was established. The SSLM's objective was to fight for separation and total independence of the South Sudan.

That war was successfully resolved in 1972 at the Addis Ababa Peace Agreement that was meditated by Emperor Haille Selassie of Ethiopia. Conversely, the South was granted autonomy instead of complete independence. However, after the American oil company, Chevron discovered oil reserves in 1978 in the southern part of the country, this agreement slowly started to vanish. The Arab-dominated government in the North began to breach the agreement in order to control the newly discovered oil in the South and to annex areas with oil reserves to the North. As stated in the *Middle East Quarterly*, "Chevron's oil discoveries in the South led the central Sudanese authorities to renege on this Peace Agreement, redrawing provincial borders and creating a new 'Unity' province around the main oil fields" (Deng, 2001). The Sudan government eventually dishonored the agreement leading to another war against the people of the South.

The failed 1972 Addis Ababa Agreement-which ended the first civil war that erupted in 1955, is one of a litany of dishonored accords. Under this agreement, a force of 6,000 rebel soldiers was supposed to be stationed in the South for five years, then integrated into the Sudanese army. But Sudan's military ruler, Gaafar Nimeiri, ordered the soldiers to be transferred north, sparking a mutiny three years later in 1975. From that point, relations between the warring parties deteriorated until the final abrogation of the accord in 1983. (*The African Times, 2003*)

THE BEGINNING OF THE SECOND CIVIL WAR IN SUDAN

The Sudan's second civil war broke out once again after the Sudan's former President Ja'far Muhammad Numeirie came into power. "The conflict resumed in 1983 when the Khartoum government unilaterally abrogated the Addis Ababa agreement, divided the South into three regions, reduced the powers of the regional governments, and imposed Shari'a on the whole country, including the non-Muslim South" (Deng, 2001). The former President also had increased the pace of Islamization and Arabization of the South. Deng explains, "The northern-dominated government in Khartoum sought to Arabize and Islamize the South. It had two motives: a belief that homogenizing the country would ensure national unity and a desire to spread what they considered to be a superior civilization" (2001). Once again, Southerners became extremely frustrated and dissatisfied with the president's plan coupling with "Discontentment with the growing inequality and marginalization of the mass that historically led to uprisings and rebellions as different groups in different regions demand redress of historical injustice" (Deng, 2001).

Furthermore, on May 16, 1983, the Sudanese Army attacked one of its own units of the former Any-anya guerrillas incorporated into the national army after the 1972 Peace Agreement; Battalions 105 and 104 stationed in the Southern towns (Bor and Ayod) after they disobeyed the order to move to the North. As stated, "The rebellion was triggered when the government attempted to transfer southern battalions to the North, thereby removing their capacity to resist" (*The Nation, 2007*). Consequently, "Throughout April and May 1983 more and more police and soldiers deserted their units for the bush. It needed only an overt action by Khartoum to push all of these groups together into an active alliance" (Johnson, 2003). These incidents led to the formation of the Sudan People's Liberation Movement and the Sudan People's Liberation Army (SPLM/SPLA) headed by late Dr. John Garang. "The South fought under the leadership of the Sudan People's Liberation Movement and its military wing, the Sudan People's Liberation Army (SPLM/SPLA)" (*The Nation, 2007*).

PROBLEMS AND DIVISIONS WITHIN THE MOVEMENT DURING THE STRUGGLE

Unlike the first Anya-nya movement which aimed for the separation of the South, the SPLA declared it was not fighting for the same objective. It wanted to fight for the unified secular and democratic Sudan since the SPLA considered itself as a vital part of the struggle of all the marginalized groups in Sudan. John Garang, leader of SPLA/SPLM repeatedly called for national constitutional conference to agree on a secular and democratic constitution in the whole country. For instance, during the 1992 Peace talk between the Sudan government and the Southern rebel factions that was held in Nigeria's capital, Abuja, delegations from both Nasir and Torit factions presented different objectives."The Torit faction preferred a secular, decentralized, united Sudan as first option, while the Nasir faction publicly declared itself in favor of complete independence" (Johnson, 2003). The peace talk failed to materialize because government was not willing to accept any of these demands while the two factions were neither interested to give up individual's objective.

Many people had speculated that John Garang had called for liberation of the whole Sudan in order to bring onboard people from other regions in Sudan to fight together with the rebels against the regime. Since Garang did not reveal his ulterior plan, both rebel fighters and civilians became reluctant and confused over the objective of the movement. As a result, many leaders started to raise questions regarding the objective of liberating the whole Sudan, and that eventually posed internal problems after it was widely rejected by several leaders within the movement. Given that there was no outright agreement on the objective of the movement since leaders failed to address the issue through peaceful dialogue, and power struggle was beginning to emerge between prominent leaders from various groups. Thus, the movement divided itself into factions and eventually along tribal lines on the matter whether the whole Sudan need to be reformed and remains united or the South should seek a total independence from the North. This internal conflict within the SPLA reached its catastrophic point after a break-away group known as the "Nasir faction" led by Dr. Riek Machar Teny and Dr. Lam Akol called for the overthrowing of John Garang. Hutchinson states, "The Sudan People's Liberation Army (SPLA)–split into two warring factions in August 1991" (2001). The leaders of Nasir faction wanted to replace Garang and revised the objective of the movement with aim to abandon all aspirations for a united secular state and called for a new objective to fight for separation of the South and also for the implementation of democratic system within the movement as Machar and Akol accused John Garang of lacking democracy in the movement. Nevertheless, these new leaders failed to depose Garang, but revitalized the principle of "Self-Determination" where the separation began to take priority over the unity. In spite of their differences, Dr. Garang and Dr. Machar ultimately merged their forces for the sake of fighting against their real enemy (North Sudan). On the other hand, many people from Dinka ethnic group until this day perceive this unification as weakness and failure of Nuers' leadership. However, Nuers see it differently since they were preoccupied with inspirations of liberating the South Sudan and its people from tyranny regime in Khartoum as they were the first ethnic groups who disapproved unfair government policies toward the Southerners; and were also the first people to revolt against the regime in Khartoum due to that ill-treatments of the Southerners and were the first to call for the separation of the South from the North. In fact, Nuers come from an egalitarian society; therefore they never allow anyone from their own community or from outside to impose anything on them against their will. That was why they fought vigorously against the British during the colonial period and it took British more than a decade to conquer Nuers.

So, their quest for freedom from the North Sudan reflected their beliefs and norms.

PROBLEMS WITH JOHN GARANG'S OBJECTIVE OF SECULAR SUDAN

John Garang and Salva Kiir wanted to liberate the whole country and create a new Sudan that would remain united. While the Arab-dominated government claimed Sudan an Islamic and Arab state justifying that the country should be headed by a Muslim and Arab president. These limitations made it impossible for the non-Muslims, particularly anyone from the Southern regions to become the head of the state. In any case, a secular Sudan would enhance inequality and discrimination by the Northerners-dominated government. Hence, that objective was an unfavorable choice for people of South Sudan since they had been under North's brutal and unjust system since the independence. Those issues ruled out Garang and Kiir's objective for secular Sudan. Accordingly, nothing else would benefit South Sudanese people other than having their own independent state free from the Arab-North's domination.

MACHAR'S OBJECTIVE OF SELF-DETERMINATION AND INDEPENDENT STATE

Contrary to John Garang, Machar and Akol's objective was different from that of their former boss. These emerged new leaders wanted to liberate only the South. During the declaration of their split in August, 1991, Machar announced that "The SPLM/SPLA's new objective is to obtain the independence of the Southern Sudan" (Johnson, 2003). This goal of creating an independent state gained widespread support among the South Sudanese people. The objective became the best alternative for total freedom, peace, equality, development, and justice for the people of South Sudan and worth fighting for. Meanwhile, in the North Sudan, it was viewed as a debacle since the country's economy wholly relies on the South where natural resources are located. Thus, separating the South from the North would impose profound economic disaster for the people in the North.

Moreover, for the United States and other external neo-colonial governments, they insisted the transformation and the democratization of the whole Sudan would only come through Southern rebels (SPLA), the objective which John Garang stood for. Likewise, African leaders feared that splitting Sudan into two states would create dreadful unintended consequences in the entire continent. They predicted that citizens in different African countries would follow this model and they would take up arms to fight their existing governments in order to create their own independent states. Consequently, African leaders were not interested to support the separation of the South Sudan from the North Sudan. Johnson explains, "The African support for the separatist movement was virtually non-existence, whereas there were some governments who were likely to be sympathetic to a 'national liberation movement'" (2003). Similar to the United States, most African leaders were strongly supporting the objective of creating a new Sudan where it could be transformed as whole. This aim became noticeable from Ethiopian government's standpoint, which was a strong ally of the SPLA/ SPLM. As explicitly explained,

> Ethiopia interests, also, would not have been served by the Southern separation. Ethiopia wished to see Nimeiri go, but it was also fighting against its own separatists. Clearly, it would not support the precedent of dismembering its own neighboring state. (Johnson, 2003)

Therefore, the objective of creating independence South Sudan was widely rejected by the people of Northern Sudan, African leaders, and the United States. Their previous rejection to create an independent state of the South Sudan had resulted in prolonging the war and sufferings of the people of the Southern Sudan for decades.

THE AFTERMATHS OF INTER-CONFLICTS

In the midst of turmoil in the movement, many prominent leaders lost their lives due to the internal fighting between separatists and unionists. Among them were Samuel Gai Tut, AKwot Atem, William Nyuon Bany, Kuribino Kuanyin Bol, Joseph Oduho, and many others. Their deaths had brought profound setbacks in the struggle and were gravely felt by the people of South Sudan. In addition, civilians suffered tremendously and many of them lost their lives due to this conflict brought upon by the split in the movement. Hutchinson states, "Southern Sudanese civilian populations have been trapped in a rising tide of 'ethnicised', South-on-South, military violence ever since the leadership struggles began within the main southern opposition movement" (2001). This internal fighting among rebel factions over the objective of the movement brought an enormous impediment in the movement and derailed its goal for many years. As a result of internal fighting, many government towns previously captured by the SPLA were recaptured and reoccupied by the Sudanese armed forces.

> The split in the SPLA, and the material support that Khartoum offered the Nasir faction, enabled the government to regain the military initiative in many part of the South. (Johnson, 2003)

Ultimately, the merging of Nasir and Torit factions has encouraged Southerner rebels to leave behind their differences. They managed to unite their forces and agreed to fight for the objective of the "Self-determination" where people of the South would be allowed to decide either to vote for separation or unity in a referendum. Thereafter, the Sudanese Peoples Liberation Army (SPLA) gained strength and received support from neighboring countries such as Ethiopia, Eritrea, Kenya, and the Uganda. These countries provided military aid while the United States provided financial aid after it developed interest in the South Sudan's oil and other resources contrary to their previous stand on the conflict and the objective. The Unites States and various African countries gave tremendous support to the Southerner rebels after the two factions (Torit and Nasir) merged their forces and agreed to fight for Self Determination.

SANCTIONS ON SUDAN AND INTERNATIONAL INVOLVEMENT IN THE SECOND CONFLICT

While there were existing oil exploration and extraction contracts awarded to the Chinese and other Asian companies under Khartoum regime, the United States wanted to snatch up these contracts if the South separate from the North Sudan. Thus, the U.S. began to turn its back on the Sudan government and built a relation with the Southern rebels. Consequently,

> Sudan has become the target of increasingly strident rhetoric by various portions of the U.S. policymaking establishment, most notably the House Subcommittee on Africa and the State Department's Africa Bureau. Specifically, the end of the Cold War has intensified a growing perception within the U.S. policymaking establishment that Islamic fundamentalist regimes constitute threats to U.S. interests on the African continent, including in the Horn of Africa (Schraeder, 1993).

Whereas,

> Many officials privately note, for example, that the decline and fragmentation of the Soviet Union and communism have created a power vacuum in the Horn of Africa that easily could be filled by 'radical' forms of Islamic fundamentalism, such as the 'shia' variant espoused by Iran." In a statement indicative of this growing concern, a senior-level Bush administration official noted that the "march of Islamic fundamentalism" was "the single most worrisome trend for policymakers. U.S. officials were telling reporters that Sudan might become a base for exporting Islamic revolution across Africa . . . although some nongovernment specialists doubted that

11

troubled Sudan would prove very useful to the fundamentalist cause over the long term" (Schraeder, 1993).

With all the above allegations and speculations in regard to Sudan, Washington became very infuriated with the regime in Khartoum coupling with that government's relentless atrocities it had committed against the people in the South. Not to mention "The growing concern with Islamic fundamentalism—exacerbated by public disclosures that the World Trade Center bombing in New York City in 1993 was carried out by individuals associated with 'radical' fundamentalist groups in Egypt" (Schraeder, 1993). Thus, the United States included Sudan into the list of terrorist sponsoring states, and at the same time imposed various sanctions on the country. The regime became internationally isolated and suffered severe economic sanctions. Its senior officials were also banned from travelling abroad as well. Quite the opposite, with the beginning of oil drilling and pumping in 1999, revenues from the oil once again had revived the Sudan's economy. So, the Sudan government acquired more sophisticated weaponry from countries such as Russia, China, Iraq, and Iran. The brutal regime in Khartoum ultimately regained strength and meritoriously employed newly acquired weapons against the rebels and civilians in the South.

On the contrary, in the after mass of 1998 bombings of two US embassies in Nairobi, Kenya, the United States claimed to have a legitimate reason to retaliate militarily against the northern Sudan government on a pretext that terrorist master-mind, Osama Bin Laden had lived in Sudan two years prior to the bombings. As seen in the past, there have been many examples of more powerful countries invading powerless ones in order to justify their violent actions against them. Thus, Bill Clinton, the United States President at the time ordered a cruise missile attack on alleged chemical factory in Khartoum killing one person and destroying the factory. The United States had targeted that pharmaceutical company on accusation that the company was being used by terrorists for weapons manufacturing; the action that was contradictory to Washington's support for the Sudan government in the war against Southern rebels prior to the fall of the Soviet Union since the United States was providing financial support to Sudan government during the cold war era. However with deteriorating relation with the Sudan as well as losing interest from the regime, the US had to changed the course and became supporter of the rebels in the South.

THE ROLE OF CHINA AND RUSSIA IN THE SUDAN'S SECOND CONFLICT

China and Russia had sabotaged the peace process between Sudan government and Southerner rebels. After American Oil Company, Chevron was forced out from Sudan due to sanctions imposed on the country by the United States government; Chinese Oil Companies quickly went into Sudan and began oil drilling in the Southern region. Bosshard explains, "China invested in Sudan's oil exploration after several Western investors pulled out of the country because of the atrocities committed in the civil war between North and South Sudan" (2007).

In order to protect its investments, the Chinese government was not interested in ending the civil war in Sudan. It repeatedly opposed the United Nations Security Council to impose sanctions on the Sudan government for atrocities it committed against civilians in the South. Carmin and Agyeman explain, "For access to Sudan's oil fields, China vetoes or dilutes UN initiative to hold Sudan accountable for its ongoing human rights abuses" (2011). The Chinese government fears that if the war in Sudan ends and the country splits in two States, its oil companies would no longer operate in the country. The move that would jeopardize its lucrative investments since oil reserves are mostly located in the South. It also feared that its oil companies would be expelled from the newly founded nation and be replaced by United States' oil companies. Therefore, for China, it envisaged that its huge oil investments would be at risk if Sudan split in two states, a decision that it did not support.

China also benefits from the sale of military equipments to Sudan government. "In 1995, China sold six or seven F-7M fighter jets to Sudan, and there are claims that Chinese military equipment has been used in attacks on civilians in Darfur" (Bosshard, 2007). The Chinese government was also blamed for taking part in human rights abuses by cooperating with the Sudan government in dislocating farmers from its oil concession areas and the destruction of their ecosystems. As Carmin and Agyeman explain, "China has also been criticized for arming Sudan, heightening internal displacement there, and underwriting Sudan human rights abuse" (2011). Accordingly,

> China's involvement in Sudan entails both political and economic collaboration. China is reportedly desperate to secure oil sources over the long term to fuel its development efforts, which explains the several billion dollars invested in Sudanese infrastructure, including airports and dams. Likewise, it is one of the primary arms suppliers to the government of Sudan. It follows that it is in China's interest to continue sale of arms to Sudan, and for the Sudanese government to stabilize the security of the oil fields. (Switzer, 2002)

The paragraph below also give further explanations of destructions inflicted on the environment and civilians in relation to environmental injustice in South Sudan due to Chinese oil companies' operations in the country that,

> Leads to soil erosion and the loss of all the benefits associated with good soil, including agricultural productivity. Displacement The involuntary migration of communities is associated with loss of livelihoods. The loss of farmlands, grazing lands and fishing grounds brought about by displacement reduces people to begging and results in acute structural poverty. There is also a loss of cultural heritage as a result of damage to archaeological, historical and cultural sites. The abrupt relocation of rural communities into urban areas also results in cultural shock, leading to conflict between the Northern Islamic cultures and the Nuer/Dinka traditional cultures in the South. (Tutdel, 2010)

Moreover, after South Sudan gained its independence, the Chinese government became more active in the South Sudan securing economic relation. It has forgotten that it shares responsibility in deaths and sufferings of people of South Sudan, both civilians and rebel fighters in collaborating with Sudan government as well as neo-colonizers during the war in the South. In addition, the Chinese government does not abide by the international human right laws. Since it does not heed to warnings from international organizations that handle human right and environmental right issues, it will continue to involve in a range of violations in the South Sudan. Therefore, it will be impractical for China to heed warning from South Sudanese leaders and not to mention that the new compradors class in South Sudan will likely take advantage of all sorts of abuses emerging from Chinese oil companies. As it is mentioned that, "The desire for profitability and the aims of economic and political elites often takes precedence over the social and environmental considerations" (Carmin & Agyeman, 2011). Hence, most of the South Sudanese government officials will only collaborate with the Chinese oil companies in the destruction of environment and other related issues rather than holding oil companies accountable for their actions. Not to mention that South Sudanese in Diasporas who are willing to raise issues to international community regarding to violations and destructions committed by the Chinese oil companies will have less voice because China itself does not abide by international regulations when it come to those matters.

Likewise, Russia blocked the UN Security Council from imposing sanctions on Sudan and it also sabotaged the peace. It also has been selling military equipment to the Sudan government and it had no interest of ending the Sudanese war either. "With a share of 77.4%, Russia was by far the most important supplier of arms to Sudan among African countries" (Switzer, 2002). All the sophisticated weapons and military aircrafts used in the killings of South Sudanese (civilians and rebels) were acquired from Russia. So, these countries' (China and Russia) actions truly justified their positions during the Sudanese conflict. Their greed for Sudan's resources and for the protection of their investments in collaborating with other neo-imperialists has contributed to sufferings of the people of the South Sudan, Nigeria, Kenya, and other countries in Africa.

Above and beyond, the United States and China compete over the control of resources and for power to dominate the world; therefore, for South Sudan to choose China as economic partner will yield much vehemence from the United States. This partnership between South Sudan and China will generate a long-term instability that will be instigated by the competition between two economic and military powers (the United

States and China). And this competition will likely disintegrate South Sudan into political turmoil and it will eventually lead to civil war that will be set off and funded by those nations. If that is the case, then, South Sudan must prepare to embrace for internal conflict attributable to resources and vested interests if its leaders continue to do business with China. For the United States, since it was a sole country that made the independence of the South Sudan possible, it will feel that its expectations and its support for the people of South Sudan has been betrayed by the people of South Sudan and its leaders, the country it helped to create. For that reason South Sudanese leaders must work very hard to maintain a strong relation with the United States and invite its companies to participate in South Sudan's reconstructions, resource explorations, and extractions to fulfill the US.'s expectations. Otherwise, it will be a grave mistake from the South Sudanese leaders to engage in all of soft of businesses deals with China while ignoring the Unites States. Accordingly, this young nation should not engage in doing business with China or Russia at all because these two countries played very destructive roles during the country's long civil war. They had prolonged the war and used to provide sophisticated weaponries to Sudan that were used in the conflict and in the killings of South Sudanese civilians. Given that they have been allies to the North Sudan thus building a relation with them (China and Russia) will create unintended consequences because their current relations with the North Sudan will threaten South Sudan's national security and its interests.

PEACE TALKS AND THE EMERGING OF THE CONFLICT IN DARFUR

With peace talks between the government and the rebels (SPLA) commenced in 2002 and various ceasefires previously in place, the war decreased dramatically in the South while another war emerged in the Darfur region. As *New African reported,* "In 2003, a rebellion led by an alliance of three ethnic groups–the Fur, the Masalit, and the Zaghawa– broke out in Darfur" (*2012*). The rebels in Darfur claimed that their region was also marginalized and demanded self-determinations similar to the ones that would be granted to the people of the South Sudan. "Fearing a similar pattern of attack from other peripheral regions, Khartoum responded with a counter-insurgency campaign throughout the region in rebel villages" (*New African, 2012*). So, President Bashir deployed his troops into the region to suppress the rebellion. He had also mobilized the Arab Janjaweed militias who later had engaged in ethnic cleansing of Black-African tribes in Darfur. In response to ethnic cleansing of Black-African in Darfur, many large protests took place around university campuses in the United States. "The administration was pressed by an unprecedented mobilization of college students and community groups, who branded Darfur "the first genocide of the twenty-first century" and insisted that the United States had a responsibility to stop it" (*The Nation, 2007*). After former Sectary of State, Colin Powell labeled "The Darfur killings 'genocide', in September 2004, the case was referred to the International Criminal Court by the UN Security Council in March 2005" (*The Nation, 2007*). The atrocities carried out by government troops and militias prompted the International Criminal Court to issue an arrest warrant for president Bashir for genocide against the people of Darfur. The International Criminal Court chief prosecutor charged President Bashir for "Intentional direct attacks on the civilian populations of the Darfur, he is being accused of five counts of crimes against humanity (murder, rape, torture, extermination, and forceful transfer of civilian population), and two counts of war crimes (killing and pillaging)" (Dagne, 2010). However, there has been no prosecution of these crimes and President Bashir is still wanted by the ICC.

COMPREHENSIVE PEACE AGREEMENT (CPA) AND REFERENDUM TOWARD INDEPENDENCE

Peace talk between the SPLA and NCP became promising. "On January, 2005, the CPA was signed by Sudan's National Congress Party-led central government and the Southern-based Sudan People's Liberation Movement/Army, ending more than two decades of war" (Dagne, 2010). The Sudan People's Liberation Army (SPLA), headed by John Garang,

"Fought four successive governments in Khartoum until, with major effort from Kenya, the United States and Europe, a Comprehensive Peace Agreement was signed "(*The Nation, 2007*).

Accordingly, People of South Sudan ought to owe tremendous gratitude to the international community such as Kenya, United States, Britain, and Norway for successfully helped in signing and implementing the Sudanese peace deal. On the other hand, there also appeared to be ulterior motives by these countries after the discovery of oil in the South. They did so in order to extract South's natural resource and engage in various businesses deals once the South split from the North. This is evident because many Kenyan and Ugandan businesses are currently operating in South Sudan as well as thousands of those countries' citizens have found work in South Sudan where they are now thriving. Many western countries' businesses are also going into South Sudan to secure business contracts. American and European Oil companies have engaged in negotiating deals with government officials to explore and extract oil and other natural resources in the country, but unsuccessful due to China snatching up all the country's oil and businesses contracts.

Moreover, many individuals also had an impact in the agreement; these various activists vigorously participated in the peace process to resolve the Sudanese conflict. Among these individuals were George Clooney, John Prendergast, the founders of *Enough Project.org* and *Sudan actionnow.org,* and actor Don Cheadle who made the movie known as *Hotel Rwanda* and *supports the organization Darfur Now.* These three activists worked tirelessly in bringing peace into Sudan both in the South and in Darfur. They brought awareness to the global policies and lobbied the United Nations and the United States government to put pressure on Sudan government so that the Comprehensive Peace Agreement (CPA) signed between Sudan government and the Sudanese People Liberation Army (SPLA) is being implemented, and the referendum is conducted peacefully and fairly. As Le Billon states, "A broader peace agreement was concluded between the Government of Sudan and the main southern rebel movement (the Sudan People's Liberation Army, SPLA) in 2005, which included oil wealth sharing and a future referendum over Southern sovereignty" (2010).

Other principles for agreement were; power sharing, Sharia laws must only be enforced in the North, and self-governance for the South followed by a referendum at the end of six years. At the end of the self-governing period in the South that began in 2005 and ended in 2010, the registration for the referendum kicked off and continued through the entire month of December, 2010. Nearly four million Southern Sudanese registered in South Sudan and in eight foreign countries, and the South Sudanese peacefully voted for separation in a weeklong referendum from January 9-15, 2011. "The referendum held on January 9, 2011, was a milestone for Sudan. With an overwhelming majority of 98.3 percent, southerners decided to secede from the north and to create Africa's youngest state-- the Republic of South Sudan" (*Middle East Time*, 2011). This referendum result was recognized by Bashir, the president of Northern Sudan and by the rest of the world. Six months later, the declaration of South Sudan's independence was officially announced on July 9, 2011. South legally becomes the Republic of South Sudan. Consequently, "The Comprehensive Peace Agreement (CPA) signed in 2005 brought an end to the brutal civil war (1955-1972; 1983-2005) that engulfed Sudan for extended periods after its independence in 1956" (Zambakari, 2012).

Unfortunately, Dr. John Garang, the leader of the Sudan People Liberation Army (SPLA/SPLM) who signed the peace agreement with the government of Sudan died in a helicopter crash just 21 days after he was sworn into office as the first Vice-President of the Republic of Sudan. As stated, "Just a few months after the CPA was signed, Garang's helicopter crashed into a mountain on the Uganda-Sudan border, in July 2005" (*The Nation, 2007*). John Garang was known as a radical Marxist whose views differed from many leaders both in the West and in Africa. The United States, Great Britain, and African leaders (particularly leaders of neighboring countries) feared that Garang would disagree with most policies imposed on his country (South Sudan) by foreign governments and that it would be difficult for foreign governments to interfere in the South Sudan's affairs. They knew that Garang was highly educated leader and knowledgeable about range of issues, thus, if John Garang would become a leader of this new nation (South Sudan) the expropriation of the country's natural resources would not be achieved by foreign corporations and influences of foreign government would not have role in the South Sudan. Therefore, individuals from those foreign governments' leaders had engineered an ulterior plan to get rid of Garang, perhaps in collaboration with one or few leaders in the country who were possibly eyeing Garang's job. Sadly, John Garang died before he could witness the declaration of the independence of South Sudan and experiences the freedom enjoyed by his people in the Republic of South Sudan, the country that he had fought to liberate from the oppressive government of Sudan for twenty-one years. The cause of the helicopter crash that has led to his premature death is still a mystery, but an investigation still ongoing to determine the cause of the crash and who involved in his tragic death.

In the same token, if Garang still alive today and remains the head of this new nation, the hysterically widespread corruptions, destitutions of civilians, and other problems that emerge due to weak government institutions and leaderships would not have occurred. At the same time former soldiers, both disabled and those whose lives vanished during the struggle would had been compensated, and their families would received money as well as other forms of compensations. It is a great shame that families of those who sacrificed their lives for this country have to live in destitutions while leaders of this country gobble up the country's wealth and use these resources for themselves and their families as they were the only people who fought for the independence of this nation. Every South Sudanese has contributed in one way or in another over the cause of many decades of war where,

> Over two million people have died as a result of the war and related causes, such as war-induced famine. About five million people have been displaced, while half a million more have fled across an international border. Tens of thousands of women and children have been abducted and subjected to slavery. By all accounts, it appears to be the worst humanitarian disaster in the world today. (Deng, 2001)

OVERVIEW OF SOUTH SUDAN

South Sudan gained its independence on July 9, 2011. It is the youngest and the 54th nation in Africa and the 193rd nation in the world. Having just emerged from a ravaged and a long civil war that lasted for four decades, this circumstance has made formal education inaccessible to scores of people in the South. This Conflict was also accompanied by massive destruction in both human and materials. Presently, there is a dire need for peace, security, food, medical services, schools, infrastructures, and other services throughout the country. In order to turn this country around, its leaders must dedicate their energies to rebuilding the country and work for the benefit of helpless citizens who have nothing else to depend on other than for the government to provide social services. Accordingly, leaders of this new country must invest intensively in the country's human capital so that South Sudan has a well-qualified workforce necessary to build a strong nation.

Since almost all South Sudanese were born into war and many of them have never been exposed to a formal education quite the opposite to people in other parts of the world, the place to begin is to offer a comprehensive education free for all citizens beginning from the primary school to the higher education. The scarcity of educational opportunities throughout the region attributable to the war led adolescents and children trekked across the vast swamps and grasslands of South Sudan for weeks or months to very far distances such as Ethiopia, Kenya, Uganda, and other countries in search of education. For those remained in the country during the war, it has been difficult for them to obtain a formal education. These groups were unable to learn how to read and write both in the Arabic and in the English language with exception of some local languages. As a result, "73% of men and 84% of women are illiterate" (www. *Sudan tribune.net, 2012*). To eradicate the high percentage of illiteracy thus South Sudan government should make education a priority for the next fifteen to twenty years so that new generations can acquire formal education and hopefully align with world standard.

Like many children around the world, South Sudanese children keen to go to school to obtain education. They also dream of being doctors, engineers, teachers, and other professions. However, having access to educational opportunities in order to achieve those dreams became a big challenge. The United Nation High Commission for refugees tried to bring education to South Sudanese children who lived both in the remote areas in the South Sudan and in refugees' camps but success had been limited due to lack of qualified teachers. Instead, many of these children were forced into becoming child soldiers by the Sudan People Liberation Army (SPLA) and fought alongside the rebels in the civil war. *Christian Science Monitor* explains,

> An estimated 300,000 children under age 18 fight in armed conflicts around the world, despite the UN Convention on the Rights of the Child—ratified by 191 nations—prohibiting states from recruiting children under age 15. Here in Sudan, some 10,000 children under 18 augment the ranks of the Southern People's Liberation Army (SPLA), which has been fighting a war of independence from the Islamist government for 18 years. (Harman, 2001)

These children and their families were misled by SPLA rebels that they would be taken to schools in refugee camps in neighboring countries. Given that their parents were also eager to put their children into schools, they were willing to believe what they were told and allowed the SPLA to take their children since SPLA was thought to be the only reliable authority in the South. Nonetheless, educational opportunities promised to these children were not fulfilled; instead, they were conscripted into the rebels armies as of members of the so called "Red Army" (Jech- Amer) and kept in camps under the SPLA command. They were only trained how to shoot and how to perform maintenance on their weapons. Their commanders randomly selected those who were strong enough to carry Ak-47s and shifted them to actual training camps where they were trained and integrated into the main rebel's army upon completion of military training. As a result, these children ended up fighting alongside the rebels' armies, making Sudan one of the countries with the largest number of child soldiers. Overtime, these children were given a named known as the "Lost Boys and Girls of Sudan".

> A group of 20,000 young boys formed, wandering the desert seeking safety. They became known as the 'Lost Boys of Sudan.' The boys crossed hundreds of miles of desert. They faced enemy fire, lion attacks and hunger. Thousands died along the way. The

survivors found safe haven in UN refugee camps in Ethiopia and then Kenya. (Witthoft, 2007)

After an attempt to locate their parents and could not find whereabouts because they (parents) were either killed in the war or were displaced to various countries, the United Nation decided to give them a second life with support from the United States. These orphans or the "Lost Boys and Girls" of Sudan were allowed to resettle in the United States through the United Nation Refugees Resettlement program. Witthoft states,

> With peace in Sudan unforeseeable and without family or opportunity in the camp, the US government decided to bring the 'Lost Boys' to America. In 2001, four thousand of the boys, who are now young men, were given high priority refugee status and began settling all across America. (2007)

Upon arriving in the United States, many of these "Lost Boys and Girls" found work to support themselves and their relatives in South Sudan and in other countries in Africa; whereas many of them have been attending schools and have successfully achieved their education, ranging from high school diplomas to Master's degrees and few are pursuing their PHDs here in the United States.

MY STORY

My educational endeavor was inspired by my late uncle (Gatluak Ruach) who pursued his education both in Sudan and in the neighboring country (Ethiopia) during Sudan's first civil war in 1960s-1970s. Like rest of few educated Southerners, my late uncle joined the first movement along with my father and both became Anya-nya rebel that fought against the government of Sudan. Since there were only few people from the South Sudan who had learned English at school because Arabic was the national language at the time, my late uncle became one of a small number of South Sudanese who went to school to learn both languages (Arabic and English). So, as a little boy, I remember when I used to sit next to him and I would imitate him when he was reading in English. That experience has left a positive and permanent impression on me. Not to mention that I have been inspired by acquiring knowledge and striving to become one among individuals who continue for success in education.

Linking my educational pursuit to the situation in South Sudan as it resembles to the "Lost Boys and Girls" of Sudan and many others South Sudanese stories, thus, I was born into war and began primary education in the war torn region of Sudan (now South Sudan) in Nyangore (Nyangore Payam), Ulang County, Upper Nile state. In the midst of civil war between Sudan people Liberation Army (SPLA) based in South and the North's dominated government in Khartoum, schools in the South were destroyed; teachers had fled to North Sudan and neighboring countries while others had joined the rebellions. These circumstances had created limited access to education for anyone in the southern regions. Consequently, people in the South had to look for education elsewhere, therefore, I became one of those who left for neighboring countries and beyond in search of education.

In the late summer of 1987, at the age of 12, I left my parent behind in our village for search of education in Ethiopia. I trekked a long and an exhausting journey for weeks from Ulang County, South Sudan to Itang refugee's camp in Ethiopia, a home for hundreds of thousands of South Sudanese Refugees who had fled from the war in Sudan. It was wearisome journey since it was during the rainy season and all rivers and lakes were over flooded by water that was running down from Ethiopia's Highland. The floods made it difficult to cross and to walk vast areas of swamps and lakes. Some lakes and rivers were so deep that one had to swim across for several minutes. After more than two weeks of exhausting journey, I had finally arrived at Itang Refugee camp and received by relatives who stayed in the camp. Two months later, I had enrolled in an accelerated English language school sponsored by a local church. The curriculum consisted of Basic English and Math; each class lasted for duration of three months. I attended it for a year and passed all my classes and became eligible to enroll in summer course program. This course covered 6th grade materials and it prepared students for an entrance exam so that one could be eligible to enroll in Ethiopian government-sponsored school that provided classes from 7th grade and beyond. After completion of summer course, I and other South Sudanese Refugee students were given an entrance exam to 7th grade. So, I passed the Entrance Exam and fulfilled all requirements for admission into Ethiopian government-sponsored school along with few other students including some of my childhood friends.

My acceptance into government-sponsored school became a turning point and a stepping stone in my educational pursuit. I enrolled in the Ethiopian government- sponsored school and I continued my education at Itang Elementary and Secondary School up to 8th grade. I attended it for two years before I could be transferred to Gambella Secondary School to attend 9th grade under the sponsorship of the United Nations Educational Programs. Conversely, in the summer of 1991, my study was briefly interrupted after the collapse of Ethiopian-Dergue regime. All South Sudanese refugees who lived in refugee camps and in several other towns in Ethiopia fled back to Sudan (South Sudan) due to fear of vengeance from new regime because the South Sudanese rebels were fighting alongside Ethiopian's troops against its rebels. So, after crossing over the border into Sudan, we encountered with heavy bombardments from Sudanese warplanes (Russian made-Antonove and Migs). We were easy prey and vulnerable because we were travelling in large numbers without any sort of security protection either from UN or from any other entities. To justify its attacks when confronted by the United Nations, the Sudan government allegedly claimed that we (refugees) were not civilians but a SPLA rebels, a claim that was completely false. The bombardments continued throughout our entire journey until we had arrived in our respective towns and villages inside Sudan. Fortunately, most of those bombs had landed in Sobat River or in swarm areas with minimal casualties. I arrived safely in my village (Nyangore) and stayed there with hope that I would find a mean to go to North Sudan or to Kenya in order to continue my studies. Two months passed without any success in my attempt since it was impossible to travel either to Kenya or to North Sudan due to insecurity and lack of transportation. After a brief stay with my parents, I left them behind again as soon as news reached us that new regime in Ethiopia had restored peace and security and it was allowing South Sudan refugees into Ethiopia.

I trekked again to Ethiopia and arrived at Itang Refugees camp after more than a week. While in transit camp, we were faced with resentment from Anuaks (tribe that lives along Ethiopia/Sudan border). Anuaks were reluctant to allow South Sudanese refugees particularly those from Nuer tribe into Ethiopia due to tribal tension that had built up over many years. They wanted to suppress the Nuers influx into Ethiopia with an intention of preventing Nuers population from rising since the two tribes have been involved in dispute as well as power struggle over a shared region (Gambella). Prior to the collapse of the Dergue regime, the Sudan People Liberation Army (SPLA) used to provide security for refugees living in camps in Ethiopia, but SPLA was expelled by the new regime. Anuaks grasped security vacuum and preyed on vulnerable refugees. They attacked Nuers both in camps and on roads from Itang to Gambella and in other areas. They used to set up check points and searched vehicles for Nuer passengers, abducted them at the gun point, and took them into thick forest where they would eventually be executed. These attacks led to loss of many lives, including my own relatives whom we left together from our village in South Sudan. A prominent pastor from Seventh - day Adventist Church who was also from Nuer tribe lost his life in the hands of Anuaks. Pastor Gatwech Wuol was very humble man who had dedicated his entire life doing God's work. Late Pastor Wuol used to provide training and offered English classes at his church for many South Sudanese Refugees including myself. He had educationally inspired many Nuer youth both in the camps and beyond.

We were habitually subjected to harsh treatments and lived in fear both at Itang Refugees Camp and in Gambella. After those painful months of waiting in vain, we were eventually transferred to Kaffa region in North-Western part of Ethiopia once the United Nations educational officer realized that Gambella region was not a safe place for us due to threats from the Anuaks. To leave from Gambella, we had to be escorted by Ethiopian soldiers due to fear of being killed on the roads. Once in Kaffa region, I enrolled in Bonga Comprehensive Secondary School along with other South Sudanese refugee students and attended it for one semester. However, over the midterm break, all South Sudanese Refugee students who attended that school left for capital city, Addis Ababa, to protest at the United Nations Educational Program headquarter; our intention was to ask for an increase of allowances but the United Nations Educational Program officer was exasperated by our actions, and later decided to terminate our scholarships and dismissed us from the program. After expulsion from Educational programs, I had no other means of paying for school I could not find another sponsor. Therefore, I opted to travel to Kenya in anticipation that I would find opportunities to continue my studies. I took a bus from Addis Ababa to the border town of Moyale and spent two days at the border to obtain immigration clearance before I could proceed to Walda refugee camp. After receiving admission from Kenya's immigration office at the border, I proceeded to Walda camp where I united again with some of my former classmates who were also expelled from the program.

Once again, I found myself living in the refugee camp for the second time. We (South Sudanese) together with the Somali, Ethiopians, and the Congolese refugees shared that desert camp and lived there under sweltering heat for several months. Again, I found that there was no educational opportunity for me in Kenya; so, I had to focus on getting resettlement to the United States or other western countries through the United Nations Resettlement program. Nonetheless, after spending eight months in Walda camp, South Sudanese refugees clashed with Somali refugees resulting in loss of many lives from both sides. Unfortunately, one of my former classmates lost his life in that clash. Consequently, all South Sudanese had to be relocated to IFO Refugee Camp in Garissa district in North-Eastern Kenya. Luckily, I resumed the resettlement processes in IFO camp. After staying idly in refugee camps in Kenya for two and half years, I was finally accepted by the United States government under the sponsorship of International Rescue Committee (IRC).

In the late September 1994, I took along flight from Nairobi, Kenya to United States. I landed first in New York and took another flight to my final destination in Dallas, Texas where I had stayed for 3 months before I moved to Atlanta, Georgia to look for better opportunities. Once in Atlanta, I was offered a job at Hyatt Hotel with the help of Lutheran Social Services. Then, I became occupied with work and getting accustomed to a new life in the United States. However, my busy schedule at work did not stop me from enrolling into an Adult Learning Center where I attended evening classes. I spent 6 months in Atlanta and moved again to Nashville, Tennessee in order to reconnect with childhood friend or classmate (Mai Chuol) and others from South Sudan. While staying in Nashville, I took a job at a food processing facility which produced food for the State of Tennessee's detention centers. I worked at that facility for a year. I was also taking high school classes from a Correspondence School in Pennsylvania. Given that I was doing entry level jobs for those first 2 years, I realized that it was not suitable for me. So, I developed an interest in job skill training and moved back to Atlanta in 1997 in order to attend a vocational school to become a Computer and Electronics Service Technician. I completed the program after 9 months and I was offered a job at Vitel Technologies, Inc., and then at Scientific-Atlanta, Inc. I worked at both companies as a Computer and Electronic Technician and used some of the money I earned from work to support my parents and relatives whom I have left behind in the war torn region of Sudan.

Due to overwhelming aspiration to acquire more education, I enrolled again in General Educational Diploma (GED) preparatory classes at an Adult Education and Technical College (DeKalb College) in Atlanta, Georgia while I was working full time. After 6 months of self-studying and taking tests, I finally passed all GED exams. I received my GED and 500 dollars scholarship to attend DeKalb College. I studied at DeKalb College for three semesters while I was working fulltime as well. Afterward, I became interested in pursuing a degree in Electronic Engineering since education was the main reason that compelled me to seek resettlement here in the United States. So, I applied at South Dakota State University (SDSU) at Brookings, and I was accepted into the Electronic Engineering program. I move again from Southern part of the United States to the Midwest in the falls of 2001 to attend SDSU where I attended it only for one semester because the school was charging higher tuitions since I was not a resident of the South Dakota at the time. Due to higher cost of tuitions, I had to withdraw from the SDSU and temporary relocated to state of Nebraska to take classes at Metro Community College in Omaha where I paid for my classes with money that I had earned from a temporarily work at UPS in Omaha.

Conversely, my life took a drastic turn after the September, 11, 2001 tragedy. I suddenly stopped my studies and enlisted in the United States Military in the spring of 2002 and left for Basic Training at Fort Jackson, South Carolina. After completion of 6 months of intensive military training, I returned to Midwest and attended Minnesota State University in Mankato while serving in the Army's reserve. However, within three months after I returned from training, the United States government declared war on Iraqi government in March, 2003. In order to justify the invasion, President George W. Bush accused the Iraqi government of having links with a terrorist organization (Al-Qaida) and that Iraq had Weapons of Mass Destruction (WMD). Therefore, our unit was called up for deployment in support of the Operation Enduring Freedom (OEF). So, I was obligated to drop my classes and withdrew from MSU as required by Military obligation since it precedes all other obligations except if it is for medical reason. Thus, our Battalion, 1- 125th Field Artillery of the Red Bull Brigade was activated and deployed oversea. My unit was stationed in Italy for the duration of 8 months at Camp Darby and Vicenza Military Base. After completion of our tour, we returned to the United States in the spring of 2004. In less than a year later, we were call back again for another deployment to Iraq. We were sent for retraining for six months at camp Shelby, Mississippi before getting boots on the ground in Iraq. Upon completion of the training, we were flown into Kuwait and spent two week there for more trainings and acclimatization and flew into Iraq afterward. Once in the country, our Unit was stationed at Forward Operation Base (FOB) Scania located at the South of Bagdad, and the remaining units were stationed in other Forward Operation Bases in Iraq. Our brigade was initially deployed in the country for 12 months but after the president ordered additional troops on the ground (troops surge), the entire Red Bull Brigade was extended for additional four months. We ended up serving in the combat operation in Iraq for 16 months making the Red Bull Brigade to serve the longest in Iraq.

Due to serving in the military and being deployed twice, it had hindered me from attaining my degree on time that took nearly a decade to accomplish. Over the course of my studying as well as serving in the military, I had received many daunting advices from friends who assumed that I would not be able to succeed in education if I continue serving in the military suggesting that I should give up one and only focused another. Nevertheless, with dedication and determination I have maintained the course and continued focusing on my educational ambition regardless of obstacles that I had have encountered since the beginning of my educational journey 25 years ago. I have promised to continue this journey until I arrive at my destination. Indeed, it took a considerable amount of hard work to effectively mastered schoolwork after I had engaged in non school-related activities such as combat operation under continuous threat from enemies and from a constant fear of imminent death for 16 months. However, with perseverance and purpose despite having absent from school for 2 consecutive years (an equivalent of four academic semesters) I had not hesitated to recommence my studies within less than two months after returning from combat operations. I eventually completed course works and graduated with a Bachelor's degree within 2 years after long military deployment (Operation Iraqi Freedom) where I served for 16 months in combat zone.

Furthermore, three months after I graduated from SDSU with a Bachelor's degree in Electronic Engineering, I took a long awaited trip in summer of 2009 to visit my parents and siblings in South Sudan whom we had been separated by civil war for 22 years. Upon my arrival in South Sudan, I quickly proceeded to the town where my parents reside in order to meet them. It was one of the happiest days of my life to meet again with my father, siblings, and other relatives after 22 years. On the other hand, I was sad too because I did not meet with my mother. Sadly, she passed away 12 years prior. Her death haunts me until this day because it was unfortunate that she died from a treatable disease. Her premature death could have been prevented if there was access to medical care in South Sudan. Her death at very young age was wholly attributable to civil war that had ravaged the country for many years causing so many innocent lives directly or indirectly. However, in the absence of my mother, we went ahead and held a home-coming celebration with rest of the families for many days while relatives were continuously visiting from other villages. It was a short visit and it was for only two-and half months and I had to return to the United States since I was anticipating to land on a job in engineering field and continue to support my parents. Conversely, the 2008's financial meltdown that occurred in the United States had led to the widespread unemployment causing an eventual recession. So, it became hard for new graduates to get employment even with adequate skills and education. Instead of wasting time on endless search for employment with no job in sight, I decided to return to school to pursue a Master's degree.

While exploring my field of interest, I came across the Social Responsibility Master's program offered at St. Cloud State University in Minnesota. The program is unique and the only one in the country. It offers a multidisciplinary degree in the study of Human Relations, Sociology, and Women's Studies. Thus, it fulfilled my interest in social issues locally and globally. So, I enrolled in the program in the fall semester of 2010 and continue thereafter for little over 2 years. While in the program I found my first classes in Social Responsibility filled with a mixture of enthusiasms and distress. The materials covered were shocking and at the same time informational. The issues ranged from destruction both on humans and on the environment caused by militarism, the role imperialism played in the exploitation of developing countries, the devastating effects of corporate greed and power, the atrocities committed by leaders of powerful nations against weak nations; the crimes committed by leaders against individuals in the pretext of protecting national security, and the other related issues imposing threat to individual and the society.

After learning in depth of this information, I developed much bitterness and started to question the motives behind powerful nations and their leaders in harming powerless nations and the sufferings imposed by leaders of individual nation. I became very concern that South Sudan and its people could easily become victims of these imperialist actions as well as of its own leaders. I began to worry about what could possibly happen to South Sudan once it becomes an independent state. Furthermore, I started to question why leaders have no mercy on ordinary people and why powerful nations and their leaders focus on vested interests regardless of negative consequences of their decisions and actions. With all of these concerns I chose to do further research into what may lie ahead in my birth country (South Sudan) and whether or not there is a significant and beneficial role I could play in the years to come. All these led me to conduct a research on issues that may impose threat to South Sudanese people both externally and internally.

EXTERNAL FACTORS AND CHALLENGES ON DEVELOPMENT AND DELIVERY OF SERVICES

In addition to the instability of the South Sudan government, other factors are emerging that threat the development, delivery of services, and prosperity. This young nation is at a greater risk of further destruction and exploitation from more powerful countries such as neighboring states and the Western nations. It becomes obvious that imperialist countries are intensively expanding colonization through corporations that expropriate and exploit undeveloped countries 'resources. Parenti explains, "Capitalist imperialism invests in other countries, transforming and dominating their economies, cultures, and political life, integrating their financial and productive structures into an international system of capital accumulation" (1995). The imperialist countries are going to continue plundering South Sudan's resources through neo-imperialism as long as the South Sudan leaders implement neoliberal's policies. If not heeded by the leaders of the South Sudan, the following statements will come into reality in the South Sudan's economic policies as required by the IMF and World Bank.

> First government must remove all rules and regulations standing in the way of the accumulation of profits. Second, they should sell off any asset they own that corporations could be running at a profit. And third, they should dramatically cut back funding of social programs. Within three-part formula of deregulation, privatization and cutbacks. (Klein, 2007)

The above policies had occurred in the old Sudan before the split. For instance, "The condition the US and IMF imposed on Sudan for their financial support in early 1980s was the forced reduction of state budget and privatization of nationalized corporation" (Johnson, 2003). While this economic policy is soon to penetrate into South Sudan's economic system, its agents such as transnational corporations, the World Bank, and the IMF guided by the so called the Washington's Consensus will more likely dictate South Sudan leaders in decision-makings and also in conducting their country's affairs as it has been an ongoing policy that affects third world countries. Parenti explains, "The colonized country is denied the freedom of trade and the opportunity to develop its own natural resources, markets, and industrial capacity" (1995).

South Sudan is now a confirmed member of the World Bank and the IMF after only nine months of gaining its independence. Its membership is being viewed by the average South Sudanese people and leaders as a positive step toward development. However, it will only impose undesirable consequences on South Sudan's economic policy and its development because its leaders will be forced to take unnecessary loans by these institutions which will become burden to the people of South Sudan for many generations.

Likewise, the intention of IMF and the World Bank is to destabilize economic systems in third-world countries by carrying out corporate interests as it is a case that "Much of Africa–including South Africa–has been victimized by privatization-related foreign investment" (Bond, 2006). These two sister institutions usually provide loans with strings attach to those loans and force countries to reform their existing economic systems requiring them to privatize, to globalize, to unfetter their markets through the so called fair trade or free market, and cutting of government services as requirements for implementation of their structural adjustment programs policy. As it is clearly explained below,

> To avoid default, the poor nations keep borrowing. But to qualify for more loans, a country must agree to the IMF's restructuring terms. It must cut back on domestic consumption while producing more for export in order to pay off more of the debt. The debtor nation must penalize its own population with cuts in food subsidies, housing, and other already insufficiently funded human services. It must devalue its currency, freeze wages, and raise prices so that its populace will work even harder and consume less. And it must offer generous tax concessions to foreign companies and eliminate subsidies to locally-owned and state-owned enterprises. (Parenti, 1995)

Additionally, many leaders in the third-world countries are obliged by their countries' economic needs and take higher interest rate loans. "When privatizations and free-trade policies are packaged together with financial bailout, countries have little choice but to accept the whole package" (Klein, 2007). Accordingly, "The debts of some nations have grown so enormous that the interest accumulates faster than payments can be met. The debt develops a self-feeding momentum of its own, consuming more and more of the debtor nation's wealth" (Parenti, 1995). This practice hinders development and delivery of social services to those in need while at the same time countries do not benefit from those loans.

Indeed, African nations now repay more than they receive. Economic experts believe that Sub Sahara Africa spends 25 thousand dollars every minute to creditors as a result of the debt monopoly imposed by the World Bank and the IMF. For instance,

> In 1980, loan inflows of $ 9.2 billion were comfortably higher than the debt repayment outflow of 3.2 billion, so the Ponzi scheme continued: by 2000, only 3.2 billion flowed in, and 9.8 billion was repay, leaving a net financial flows deficit of 2-6 billion" [sic]. By the early of 2000s, the debt remained unbearable for at least 21 countries, at more than 300 per cent of exporting earning. (Bond, 2006)

That practice also leaves no money for development and other services because money that is supposed to go into development is being spent on paying loans and interests for generations. Perkins explains, "The loan of foreign aid insures that today's children and their grandchildren will be held hostage, they will have to allow corporations to ravage their natural resources and will have to forego education, health, and other social services merely to pay us back" (2005). Frankly speaking, money from these loans is actually going back to western corporations, corrupted state officials or what Parenti calls the compradors class and the military that protect the interests of governments and corporations rather than going to concrete development. It is obvious that, "Most of the Foreign aid never reaches the needy segments of the recipient nations. Much of it is used to subsidize US. Corporate investment and substantial amounts finds its way into the coffers of corrupt comprador rulers. Some of it subsidizes the cash-crop exports of agribusiness at expense of small farmers who grow food for local market" (Parenti, 1995).

Parenti further explains that,

> The comprador class is well recompensed for its cooperation. Its leaders enjoy opportunities to line their pockets with the foreign

aid sent by the U.S. government. Stability is assured with the establishment of security forces, armed and trained by the United States in the latest technologies of terror and repression. (1995)

What has been mentioned above is ongoing practice in South Sudan and will even get worst in coming years unless new government is formed that will take initiative to reform and create strict regulations to prevent those practices. Furthermore,

Since the World War II, the US. Government has given over $200 billion in military aid to train, equip, and subsidized more than 2.3 million troops and international security forces in some eighty countries, the purpose being not to defend them from outside invasions but to protect ruling oligarchs and multinational corporation investors from the dangers of domestics anti-capitalist insurgency. (Parenti, 1995)

Similarly, "Arms are sold to almost any country with money to buy them or given to selected governments through foreign aid programs" (Andrzejewski, 2009). Therefore, similar economic foreign aid policies will ruin South Sudan's political and economic system and it will impose despair once implemented.

It is apparent that neoliberalism is indeed a mean to exploit and bankrupt Third World countries. "The legacy of imperial domination is not only misery and strife, but an economic structure dominated by a network of international corporations which themselves are beholden to parent companies based in North America, Europe, and Japan" (Parenti, 1995). Parenti further explain that, "The process of expropriating the natural resources of the Third World began centuries ago and continues to this day" (1995).

South Sudan is not exempt from this destruction Therefore, this country and its people will be among the countries affected by those policies. Imperialism will once again reveal itself in South Sudan as it has affected other African countries during the colonial period. Above and beyond, perpetual poverty will also engulf South Sudanese people into deep poverty because the country will be forced to depend on mono crops, and will produce only one crop for the world market while getting less for what it produces to feed its citizens. This mono crop plan is also associated with the policy of the World Bank and the IMF as it is awfully common in undeveloped and developing countries as it obvious that "Cooperative lands are supplanted by agribusiness factory farms, villages by desolate shanty towns, and autonomous regions by centralized autocracies" (Parenti, 1995). Neo-liberal policies are also imperial policies that have been designed to pillage the African continent and other global South nations. Bond clearly explains,

> The looting of Africa dates back to many centuries, to the point which value transfers began via appropriate of slave labour, antiquities, precious metals and raw materials. Unfair terms of trade were soon amplified by colonial and neocolonial relations. These processes often amount to a kind of primitive accumulation', by which capital of Northern countries grew by virtue of looting Africa. (2006)

South Sudan, a new nation that will become a victim of that policy along with other African countries that have been victimized for generation, unless its leaders become aware of this practice and make better decisions when dealing with neoliberal policies. Furthermore, people in South Sudan have survived on their own for many generations, therefore, no need for the World Bank and the IMF to advise them when extracting their resource or farming their lands. If they are left alone they will do better on their own as they have been doing it for centuries. Hence, in any country in Africa, "The problem is not poor lands or unproductive populations but foreign exploitation and class inequality" (Parenti, 1995).

Foreign exploitation and class inequality within the country are also among problems that will face the people of the South Sudan. The gap between the poor and the rich is growing rapidly at an incredible rate in less than two years after the South Sudan gained its independence. These problems together with many other issues begin to take shape which threatens progress and prosperity in this new nation.

CORPORATION'S SOCIAL AND ENVIRONMENTAL IMPACTS

Corporations together with wars cause much of the devastation everywhere in the world today. They are account for environmental destruction, extinction of species, diseases, and deaths. These transnational corporations become predators on everything on our planet and the root causes of many problems we face in our era. They continue to exploit and alienate workers including children by subjecting them to poor working environments; they continue to produce chemicals that threaten people's health and cause deaths in many parts of the world, and they continue to pollute our environment. Whereas, "Enormous environmental damage has been created by industrialization, imperialism, and technological processes of extracting natural resources from the earth with no regard for the long-term consequences to people, animals, or the earth" (Andrzejewski, 2009). This "System of domination and resource extraction cannot be imposed or sustained without force or the threat of force" (Andrzejewski, 2009). Therefore, corporations provide tools for the military to execute wars which include; displacing, killing, and polluting the earth that result in global warming and other health related issues that threaten the survival of human, animals, and environment.

Treadmill production argues that the overconsumption in Western Industrial countries and the need for more capitals drive up production of goods which later dumped after used without conserving and restructuring them. In recent years, "It has become increasingly obvious that the looming byproducts of industrialism, the technological revolution, and hyper-consumerism threaten people's livelihood everywhere" (Andrzejewski, 2009). There are more signs about our planet coming to extinction due to climate change. Carmin & Agyeman explain, "Climate change is undoubtedly the most significant. It threats our future development and, in some people's minds, put at risk the continued existence of our own species and the global ecosystems which we depend" (2011).

Likewise, overexploitations of resources have created an imbalance in the ecosystem and deforestation threatens wild life and other species as "The world's richest nations are depleting natural resources at an unprecedented rate, mass extinction is exponentially increasing due to these manmade disasters, "and "If the current trend continue, half of the species or all will disappear forever" while "global warming could doom millions of species by 2050" (Ulansey, 2009). Additionally,

> The global human family faces enormous challenges, yet we begin to see a bigger picture and finally hearing what scientists have been telling us for years, habitat destructions, climate crises, pollutions, and another factor multiplied by growing human population are driving our fellow creatures to extinction so rapidly that an entire ecosystem may face irreversible change reaction collapse. (Stone, 2010, *Earth Days Film*)

Furthermore, in capitalist market system, it is evident that "Companies appear to follow paths of least resistance in terms of regulation because any compliance costs are believed to erode profitability" (Carmin & Agyeman, 2011). When corporations implement those strategies it creates a "Potential for environmental harm from external agents" (Carmin & Agyeman, 2011). Consequently, the United States and other western countries race to control markets and natural resources in the global south nations. As a result, "Wealth is transferred from Third World peoples to the economic elites of Europe and North America (and more recently Japan) by direct plunder, by expropriation of natural resources, the imposition of ruinous taxes and land rents, the payment of poverty wages, and the forced importation of finished goods at highly inflated prices" (Parenti, 1995). One study also finds that,

> North American and European corporations have acquired control of more than three-fourths of the known mineral resources of Asia, Africa, and Latin America. But the pursuit of natural resources is not the only reason for capitalist overseas expansion. There is the additional need to cut production costs and maximize profits by investing in countries with cheaper labor markets. (Carmin & Agyeman, 2011)

Moreover, big corporations such as Wal-Mart and Nike have relocated their production facilities in countries overseas where the cost of labor is cheap and no benefits must be paid to the workers. As explained "Transnational corporations have located their facilities in remote locations to obtain cheap labor and supply chains have reached into the far corners of the earth to obtain the raw materials that sustain global production and consumption" (Carmin & Agyeman, 2011). These corporations usually lure children to work in production lines. Instead of going to school and participate in activities which other children take for granted in countries such as United States, Canada, Australia, and European countries, they are being exploited and deprived of childhoods. For example, "In countries like Mexico, India, Colombia, and Egypt, children are dragged into health-shattering, dawn-to-dusk labor on farms and in factories and mines for pennies an hour, with no opportunity for play, schooling, or medical care" (Parenti, 1995). They are subjected to long working hours under poor conditions while exposed to various chemicals in different factories which could cause cancer and other related diseases. Parenti explains, "Imperialism forces millions of children around the world to live nightmarish lives, their mental and physical health severely damaged by endless exploitation" (1995). For children, as young as eight being in such a state could impose severe health problems ranging from emotional, mental, and physical problems that can pose long-term effects. Whereas,

> In India, 55 million children are pressed into the work force. Tens of thousands labor in glass factories in temperatures as high as 100 degrees. In one plant, four-year-olds toil from five o'clock in the morning until the dead of night, inhaling fumes and contracting emphysema, tuberculosis, and other respiratory diseases. (Parenti, 1995)

In the same way, these transnational companies are in the process to open their businesses in South Sudan; by allowing those companies to do business in this country that has no tough and effective regulation will impose negative consequences on South Sudanese people and its environment, as a result, people of South Sudan including children will be relentlessly exploited by those businesses.

Child labor is also an ongoing problem in South Sudan; however, it is taking place at the low levels and it carried out by local businesses. One article stated, "In the Unity State child labour is common, with many children walking the dusty roads looking for customers, for shoe polishing, selling goods from wheelbarrows, as well as bread and sweets to earn for living" (*http://www.sudantribune.com*, 2012). Those children perform jobs not suitable for one under the age of eighteen. Some of them are either forced by their parents to work in order to help support the family or their individual situation forced them to do so due to lack of family support. This is a failure of federal and state governments which supposed to build boarding schools and community centers in main cities and county headquarters where these children can engage in useful school related activities that can prepare them for bright future, and also at the same time, the government should provide basic services to their families. Also, Pepsi-Cola Company is currently building a large production facility in Juba, South Sudan. This company will involve in exploitation of South Sudanese children. These despaired children will more likely be subjected to exploitation and use as alternative sources for cheap labor as always a pattern for corporations unless the government of South Sudan puts policy in place that will protect children and citizens from exploitations. This perceived exploitation will be more substantial once many corporations join in and relocate their businesses in South Sudan.

In addition to child labor, adults are also being exploited and alienated by these corporations in the Third World countries. These workers have no rights at their work places and have no benefits such as medical, sick pay, and vacation which most workers have in industrial nations. Their working environments are very poor compare to ones in the industrial nations and are being subjected to harsh treatment from their bosses. The workers in the Third World work long hours and receive inadequate pay. They are generally intimidated and are unable to raise complaints regarding pay and working conditions. The individuals who raise their concerns could be subjected to disciplinary action resulting in losing one's job, which is most likely the only sole income for the entire family. This exploitation and alienation by corporations will also affect the people of South Sudan as these happen to many people in different countries in the global South.

THE USE OF CHEMICAL AND BIOLOGICAL

Corporations produce chemical and biological weapons that are being used by militaries in numerous wars. These chemicals and biological warfare once used in war usually ends up in the atmosphere and drips back to earth affecting the air, soil, water sources, and the entire ecosystem. There are now shortages of clean drinking water particularly in the global South where chemicals and biological warfare are heavily used. It becomes evident in South Sudan where destructions caused by war have endangered human, wildlife, and other species. Due to the natural habitats being destroyed, together with war-induced famine and drought, scores of animals in South Sudan have perished while others fled to neighboring countries due to many years of fighting in the region. Drought and famine in recent years become very common in South Sudan resulting in starvation for many as ecosystem has been contaminated attributable to prolonged use of weaponries in the region. Accordingly, "The impact of global warming, mass extinction, dwindling water resources, genetic contamination, famine, deforestation, depleted fisheries, as well as renewed interest in "energy crisis"—these environmental/cultural issues threaten everyone's wellbeing on local and global levels" (Andrzejewski, 2009).

Chemical companies such as Dow Chemical, Monsanto, and others have long records of dumping toxic chemicals into environment. These companies dump billions of pounds of toxins such as carbon dioxide, sulfuric oxide, mercury, and other chemicals into environment without proper disposal. For instance, one of the worst chemical pollutions incident happened in 1984, in Bhopal, India, where,

> Over 500,000 people were poisoned by approximately forty tons of toxic gases pouring into the air from chemical insecticides plant abandoned by Monsanto killing about 8,000 people in the same night. The number of death tolls eventually rose to 200,000 in the following months. Hundreds of thousands others have permanent lung, liver, kidney, and blindness where the same deadly chemical still leaking into the drinking waters and soil which continue to affect the people until today. (Huff & Philips, 2011)

There are similar cases of illness caused by pollution in oil producing states in South Sudan. Those illnesses are results of improper operations during oil drilling and extraction. Numerous people are constantly becoming sick as a result of contamination from the oil wastes leaching into water and food sources. As defined by the U.S. Environmental Protection Agency, "An environmental injustice is present when communities, groups, or individual must contend with an environmental burden that is not their making and does not reflect their preferences, or when the acceptance of hazard fails to provide significance and meaningful justice to all of the affected parties" (Carmin & Agyeman, 2011). Oil companies that operate in South Sudan are doing nothing to prevent pollution or to clean up the contamination they have created. Thus, these oil companies have specifically moved to countries such as South Sudan where regulations are absence or lenient.

THE USE OF PESTICIDES AND HERBICIDES

The intensive use of pesticides and herbicides plus other farming chemicals has increased rapidly over the last decades after the emergence of Green Revolution. This "Systematic production, utilization, and exportation of POPs and pesticides began in the post-World War era" (Pellow, 2007). Given that pesticides have been widely used due to their abilities to kill ants and insects in agricultural farms and to eliminate bacteria in food processing plants, "One of the axes of this project was the belief that heavy pesticide and fertilizer use would lead to a greater efficiencies by producing larger crop yields, particularly in nations and regions widespread of poverty and hunger" (Pellow, 2007). Therefore, these "Chemicals became an integral component of production across most major industries and became embedded in the very fabric of industry, society, human bodies, and ecosystem" (Pellow, 2007). As a result, the intensive use of these chemical have created unintended consequences in people's health and environment.

Similarly, pesticides were used by the military in wars. For instance, during the war in the Vietnam, US. troops intensively used "Herbicide

Agent Orange to destroy foliage that offered Vietcong soldiers camouflages" (Pellow, 2007). Civilian population was greatly affected resulting in millions of deaths caused by pesticides in both Vietnamese civilians and soldiers. These chemicals are also blamed for "Causing deformity in tens of thousands of children" (Pellow, 2007). It also created a considerable deforestation and left millions of others permanently ill and the entire ecosystem have been contaminated until this day. Whereas, thousands of U.S. soldiers died from Agent Orange exposure and others are still suffering from illness caused by pesticides poisoning. For instance,

> Vietnam veterans who came back contaminated by tons of herbicides sprayed Indochina are facing terminal ailments, while their children suffer abnormality high rate of birth defects (in common with children in Vietnam, though they latter endure high rate of abnormalities). Likewise, tens of thousands of veterans from the Gulf War of 1991 have succumbed to a variety of illness due to exposure to a range of war-related, lethal substance. (Parenti, 1995)

Equally, the Sudanese government is believed to have employed intensive use of chemicals in the civil war and in the bombing on the rebels and civilians in the South because symptoms similar to the ones in Vietnam were noticed among rebel fighters, local population, and in the region's ecosystem.

Also, capitalism has enhanced theses widespread practices of environmental inequality and racism. Racism becomes a driving force that influences the decisions of corporations and others institutions to sell banned persistent pesticide pollutants to agricultural farming in the global South nations. Those "Toxic chemicals are an embodiment of racism (and gender and class violence) because they are intended to produce benefits for some while doing harm to others" (Pellow, 2007). Therefore, one can not dispute the discriminatory deeds of governments, corporations, and institutions in the global North aimed against underdeveloped and poor nations in the global South because "Today the most pesticides banned for use in the United States are exported, dumped, or used throughout the global south-a clear case of global environmental inequality and racism"

(Pellow, 2007). Besides, "Indigenous communities around the globe are [sic] affected disproportionately and harmed by POPs" (Pellow 2007).

In addition, "The risks associated with pesticides exposure tend to fall on the those benefiting the least from the pesticides use….this is a pattern reported for various LCDs[lesser developed countries] in Africa, Asia, and Latin America"(Pellow, 2007).

As a result, millions of acres of land are being eroded every year in global South nations due to chemical farming creating drought and flooding which result in hundreds of thousand deaths and billions in economic loses every year. For example, "The Third World accounts for 99 percent of deaths from pesticides". [Sic] "Annually, there are more than 25 million reported cases of pesticides poisoning in the global South nations alone" (Pellow, 2007).

The transnational corporations (TNCs) export innumerable tons of pesticides in Africa, Asia, the Caribbean, and Latin America where they contaminate water system, soil, communities, and human bodies resulting in massive destructive effects. As Carmin & Agyeman state, "The way in which pesticides are used in Africa caused serious environmental and health problems much more than elsewhere" (2011). Similarly,

> The chemical toxins and other industrial effusions poured into the world's groundwater, oceans, and atmosphere by fast-profit, unrestricted multinational corporations operating in Asia, Africa, and Latin America, the devastation Third World lands by mining and timber companies and agribusiness, are seriously affecting the quality of the air we breathe, the water we drink, and the food we eat. (Parenti, 1995)

These lead to birth defect, liver and kidney diseases, brain damage, and cancer. It also kills fish, birds, and trees. "The effects of pesticides on humans health are in many cases devastating, but the damage done to ecosystems is most immeasurable in its immensity and reach" (Pellow 2007). In several developing nations, countless number of people suffers from pesticide related disease every year. For example, "The Colombia 's aerial spraying of tons of pesticides on cocoa and poppy plants in Columbia disproportionately harms indigenous people's land and health in that nation, violating their right to clean environment as it is customary under international laws" (Pellow, 2007). Similar problems will occur in South Sudan unless the government creates tough regulations against pesticide use in the country. Currently, there are agribusinesses interested in commercial farming in the South Sudan. If South Sudan government allowed these agribusinesses to engage in commercial farming in the country, it will become disastrous because these farming industries will use pesticides which are possibly banned in developed countries. It will result in severe health problems that will affect the entire population of the South Sudan.

Similarly, the rise of pesticide-laden food consumption together with fragile laws and racial prejudice creates a condition where farm-workers and their families encounter unusually high rates of pesticides related illness, poisoning, and cancer because "Both agricultural produce and livestock farm is heavily laden with pesticides and a range of persistent organic pollutants (POPs)" (Pellow, 2007). Therefore, this "Widespread contamination of ecosystems, water sources, and agricultural land is associated with wide application of these chemicals in many countries" (Pellow, 2007). Likewise, "Medical studies have revealed health association between pesticide exposure and range of reproductive health ailments, including, stillbirths, miscarriages, birth defects, infertility, spontaneous abortion, and delayed pregnancies (Pellow, 2007). Thus, by creating additional health problems for South Sudanese people who have no excess to medical care will impose long-term illnesses and cause countless deaths. As one activist puts it, "pesticides poison our bodies, our wombs, our children…our water, air, soil, and our food" (Pellow, 2007).

Additionally, the corporatization of food production usually affects small-scale famers because few agro-food industries control the food market by mass producing their food to maximize their profits. These giant corporations push out small-scale farms and turned small agricultural and livestock farms into agribusiness creating cartels within food production industries. These Agro-food industries intensively use pesticides and other chemicals in food productions chemicals and genetically modified food, the sources of food for mass production, transforming food processing systems at an extraordinary speed due to global economic and social change; such as rapid increase of population. This demand for new technologies in agribusiness and the globalization of food system consequentially affecting small-scale farmers. Whereas, the use of pesticides and fertilizers in both agricultural and livestock impose health problems leading to obesity among children and diabetes among older people. According to one studies conducted by the U.S. Centers for Disease Control and Prevention (CDC), "Researchers tested about a sample of more than 9000 individual across the United States and found pesticides in 100 percent in these individuals" (Pellow, 2007).

Likewise, small-scale farmer are forced by agrochemical firms and financial institutions such as Monsanto, Dow chemical, World Bank, and IMF to use pesticides, fertilizers, and genetically modified seeds in their agricultures and livestock farming and to produce only mono crops for export while their markets are flooded with cheap food produced by big agribusiness driving them out of market. Some of the most influential of these corporations were engaged in manufacture and sale of toxic chemicals where persistent organic pollutants chemicals remain in ground water and soil for many years and travel to a far distance polluting our ground water and surface causing health problem for individuals. Also, the agrochemical firms and financial institutions' policy in some countries also imposed disastrous consequences on small scale-farmer due to huge debts and chemicals from these firms and institutions where farmers wind up committing suicide due to burden of loans obtained from institutions and diseases caused by the use of pesticides and fertilizers.

Besides, globalization of food has also altered source of food associated with cultures. Imported food products are introduced into nations with distinctive tastes and traditions leading to local people giving up their local dietary food for foreign food which are blended with chemicals, making it tasteful and additive. For example, many countries have embraced America fast food restaurants such as McDonalds and KFC and incorporate them into their daily meals while reducing the need for traditional food that is rich in dietary organic.

WASTE DUMPING AND TRADING
IN THE GLOBAL SOUTH

Hazardous waste exported from the West is another problem facing people in several countries in the global South nations including the people of the South Sudan. This electronic-waste (e-waste) trade is known to be one-sided trade of e-wastes from the global North to the global South nations. It began after electronics and computers equipment demands and consumption proliferated in industrial nations. Once, the environmental justice groups in the Western nations become successful in lobbying governments' officials to create and to enforce strong regulations against corporations and institutions in e-waste dumping practices in the global North nations, afterward businesses such as waste management companies, corporations, and institutions designed new ways to export, sell, and dump e-wastes in the global South. One good example is what had been taking place in Indian Ocean when Somalia pirates were attacking and hijacking Western ships suspected of illegal dumping of toxic waste in the Indian Ocean near Somali's coastal lands. These Somali Pirates' initial motive was to deter foreign ships from dumping waste near Somali's coastal lands; however, they were entrapped by the new way of making quick money and continued to engage in many illegal activities such as hijackings and demanding ransoms.

These e-wastes are intentionally mislabeled "reusable goods" or "donation" to schools, hospitals, governments, and other institution in those poor countries. Because people in global South are in dire need of electronics equipment, they tend to accept these recyclable e-wastes without hesitations, hoping that these products would be useful; however, originators of these electronics products have hidden intention, to dump these toxic electronics waste in the global South nations. It is noted that "25 to 75 percent of the secondhand electronic goods exported to Africa are broken beyond repair" (Pellow, 2007). Yet, those in the global South nations received them without questions. As explained in documentary, *Ghana Digital Dumping*, "When containers of old computers first began arriving in West Africa a few years ago, Ghanaians welcomed what they thought were donations to help bridge the digital divide. But soon exporters learned to exploit the loopholes by labeling junk computers "donations", leaving men like Godson to sort it out" (Dornstein, 2009).

In order to secure easy entrance, export representatives usually bribe custom agents at ports of entry in order to allow these e-wastes shipments to reach local recycling businesses. "When computers and other electronics goods are discarded, this e-waste is often shipped to urban areas and rural villages across Asia, Africa, and Latin America where residents and workers disassembled them for sale in the new manufacturing processes or where they are simply dumped as waste" (Pellow, 2007). These toxic elements: the lead, beryllium, mercury, cadmium, polyvinyl chloride plastics (PVCs), hexavalent chromium, and brominated –flame retarded (BFTs) found in electronics and computer wastes pose major occupational and environmental health threats. The e-waste toxics contaminated ground water and the environment resulting in illness such as kidney disease, developmental effects and loss of mental ability in children due to accumulation of lead and other chemicals in ecosystems "Because each computer monitor (the cathode ray tube) contains several pounds of highly toxic materials, this practice creates a massive transfer of hazardous waste product from North to South and is responsible for harming public health and integrity of watersheds"(Pellow, 2007).

Pellow also explain that, "Every year, northern nations and corporations produce millions of tons of toxic waste from industry, consumers, municipalities, state institutions, computers and electronics products, and agricultural practices" (2007). Therefore, "Governments, consumers, and consumptive patterns are driving the movement of waste, toxics, and other hazardous material to distant locations and, in the process are having negative impacts on natural resources, environmental quality, public health, and local social and cultural dynamics" (Carmin & Agyeman 2011).

As production increases exponentially in the global North nations, so has hazardous waste that will be shipped to developing countries for dumping and trading. "Today it is estimated that nearly 3 million ton of hazardous waste from United States and other industrialized nations are transferred across international border each year and most of these waste are being shipped from Europe, the United State, and Japan to nations in

Latin America, the Caribbean, South and South West Asia, and Africa" (Pellow, 2007). And "The problem expected to worsen because e-waste is the fastest-growing stream in industrial nations" (Pellow, 2007). Therefore, "The dumping of trash, garbage, or municipal solid waste remains the most common form of environmental inequality" (Pellow, 2007). Henceforth, South Sudan will be a new frontier for this kind of hazardous waste dumping and trading unless the government is knowledgeable about these e-wastes dumping and trading and take a strong measure by tackling this practice.

IMPACT OF AIR POLLUTION

Air pollution is one more problem caused by transnational corporations. There is an estimated fifty thousand to hundred thousand deaths each year in the United States caused by air pollution. The number of people suffering from asthma has increased dramatically by alarming rates of fifty percent or more each decade due to deteriorating of air quality. According to APE report, "6.7 million children and 1.6 million adults suffer from asthma in the United States" and "More than 45 million Americans are drinking and bathing in water that is ridden with parasites and toxic chemicals" (EPA, 2007). This sort of air problem is currently a threat that faces the people in South Sudan, mainly in Juba (Capital of South Sudan) and other big cities. The poor air quality in Juba is mostly caused by lack of sanitations and burning trashes everywhere inside the city. This also coincides with unregulated vehicles emissions. Therefore, when corporations create additional air pollution in South Sudan, it will impose a bigger health threat for the citizens of the newest nation. Their health will deteriorate dramatically as a result of insufficient air quality. Thus, government need to consider regulating vehicle emissions and ban burning of trashes and heavy use of those small gasoline powered generators used by household and businesses as their sources of electricity.

WATER SHORTAGE

Nearly eighty percent of the world's rivers are affected by pollution caused by corporations' toxic waste, chemicals, and weapons used in wars such as depleted uranium. Andrzejewski states, "The world's supply of water is shrinking dangerously, raising the specter of conflict over this most vital of natural resources" (2009). This shortage of clean drinking water is particularly common in global South nations. In those Third World countries, indigenous people usually fetch drinking and cooking water from wells and rivers. They use the water from the same sources for irrigations in farming that only result in polluting their source of food.

In the capital of South Sudan, Juba, severe shortage of clean drinking water is beyond imaginable. Water trucks and water tanks owned by individuals and operated by foreigners usually supply residents with water. This water is being drawn from Nile River, the main water sources for South Sudan; it is so polluted that one could see thousands of thousands of plastic bottles and other wastes floating everywhere in the river. Yet, this water is still used in cooking and drinking by less fortunate people. The contamination of this water has serious impacts on the health of local population. Local residents who drink from Nile River's polluted water usually get diarrhea and dehydration of the body which might lead to serious illness or death. This problem is also so common in the entire South Sudan and it is continuing to impose health risk to everyone in the region unless the South Sudan Government designs new ways to purify the source of drinking water.

LAND GRABBING AND DEFORESTATION

In addition to other issues, transnational corporations' land-grabbing and land purchasing in Third World countries has becoming a major threat and it has intensified in recent years. The process is becoming a part of ongoing expansion of imperialism by the West through Multinational

Corporation. Huff & Philips explain, "Resource exploitations in Africa are not new but the scale of agricultural lands grabbing in African nations is unprecedented, becoming the new colonization of twenty-first century" (2011). And, in South Sudan, government officials and local business grab indigenous' lands and displace them from their birth places. These officials usually come from different regions. Once they relocate into towns with their families, they end up forcing out local owners from their land and occupy them which usually result in tensions fueling tribal conflicts in many town and cities.

Similarly, deforestation carried out by logging companies threatens wild life and other species due to their natural habitats being destroyed. This practice destroys indigenous' land by using up forests resulting in the destruction of environment, causing misery for people and animals due to lack of fertile and grazing land, and puts livelihoods of indigenous peoples and their resources at risk. Parenti explains, "The expansionists destroy whole societies. Self-sufficient peoples are forcibly transformed into disfranchised wageworkers. Indigenous communities and folk cultures are replaced by mass-market, mass-media, consumer societies" (1995).

Furthermore, before the transnational corporation invade lands in third world countries, indigenous people

Hunted, fished, and raised food in their jungle orchards and groves. But their entire way of life was ruthlessly wiped out by a few giant companies that destroyed the rain forest in order to harvest the hardwood for quick profits. Their lands were turned into ecological disaster areas and they themselves were transformed into disfranchised shantytown dwellers, forced to work for subsistence wages—when fortunate enough to find employment. (Parenti, 1995)

Today, "Hundreds of millions of Third World peoples now live in destitution in remote villages and congested urban slums, suffering hunger, disease, and illiteracy, often because the land they once tilled is now controlled by agribusiness firms who use it for mining or for commercial export crops such as coffee, sugar, and beef, instead of growing beans, rice, and corn for home consumption" (Parenti, 1995). These issues will face

South Sudan and its citizens because many businesses express interest in South Sudan's dense forest for the logging and agribusinesses. It will pose dreadful consequences for the people as well as the entire ecosystem.

As learned from the above mentioned corporation-made disasters, transnational corporations operate without regard to human, animal, or environmental risks. They have relocated their business in third world countries to seek cheap labor, to secure natural resources, maximization of profits, and to seek an easy path and less regulation in those countries. Carmin and Agyeman explain, "Transnational corporations have located their facilities in remote locations to obtain cheap labor and supply chains have reached into the far corners of the earth to obtain the raw materials that sustain global production and consumption" (2011).

South Sudan is not exempt from these corporate-made disasters. Thus, when these transnational corporations relocate their businesses in South Sudan it will impose huge problems on the environment, people's health, political, and economic system. As stated, "The increasing distance between those who benefit and those who must contend with environmental, health, economic, and social impact of remote demand is intertwined with rise of spatial inequalities due to global economic, social, and political institutions" (Carmin & Agyeman, 2011). People, animals, and environment will be susceptible to negligence and abuses from transnational corporations due to nonexistence regulations against these corporations. South Sudanese people will suffer tremendously not to mention their existing fragile health conditions, malnourishments, and untreated chronic diseases due to long absence of medical attentions as result of many years of war.

Referring to corporations, Marx Weber predicted that, "Individuals would feel helpless in the face of such bureaucracy in such organizations and how would we be able to solve problems of the powerless in the face of this modern bureaucracy" (Crone, 2007). Marx and Engels also described similar bourgeoisie or corporations that it (Corporation) "Chases over the whole surface of the globe. It must nestle everywhere, settle everywhere, and establish connection everywhere . . . . It creates a world after its own image" (Parenti, 1995). Furthermore, "What has emerged in the Third World is an intensely exploitive form of dependent capitalism. Economic conditions have worsened drastically with the growth of transnational corporate investment" (Parenti, 1995).

This corporate greed to maximize profits without regard to destruction they create becomes a big concern for activists and citizens. For instance, more than 200,000 people protested against the World Bank and IMF at meeting site to demand the withdrawal of the US military from Iraq. As activist Virginia Shetshedi told the InterPress Service,

> It is not just about the war. It is about the how many people die around the world because of unfair policies and actions-a large part of which are economic. So, it is not just the military injustice that we are facing. We need to connect the dots together" [sic] "we will speak out against the corporate theft of Iraq's resources and the decimation of the Iraqi economy through privatization and "free trade. (Bond, 2005)

IMPACTS OF OIL IN SOUTH SUDAN AND IN OTHER COUNTRIES

Oil companies are responsible for much of the environmental pollution and overexploitation of natural resources that create an imbalance in the ecosystem leading to environmental destructions, political and economic instabilities, and sufferings in the global south. The oil companies together with other transnational corporations are also charged for "Inequalities stemming from foreign exploration, exploitation, and investments that have been taking place for many years and in many nations" (Carmin & Agyeman, 2011). Besides, "War profiteering itself creates a formidable support system for global aggression" (Andrzejewski, 2009). For the last several years this system revealed itself in the Sudanese conflict where oil companies fueled the civil war between the government of North Sudan and the rebels in the South, contributing to the destruction of environment and death of indigenous peoples in South Sudan. Switzer explains, "Revenues from petroleum production [sic] financing the conflict, that the oilfields have become strategic targets for rebels, and that various foreign interests–China and Malaysia, and multinational corporations from Europe, North America and Asia–have interests that are not necessarily aligned with the promotion of peace" (2002).

Also, the same oil companies in collaboration with Sudanese government had engaged in deforestation, killing, and forced immigration of people in the South Sudan as they have done these evil deeds in other countries. As explained, "Many villages have been destroyed and their inhabitants displaced by government forces during oil production activities in Sudan. Displacement is carried out by the Sudan regular army infantry backed by helicopter gunships and a high-altitude Antonov bomber (acquired from Russia by the Sudanese government" (Tutdel, 2010). To make their occupation permanent, the cleared villages were used for military bases by Sudanese government so that indigenous peoples would have no chance of returning to their villages. People who lived near refineries were subjected to cruel treatment and were sometimes being rounded up and sent to jails where they would be tortured or killed.

While this young nation (South Sudan) is transitioning into becoming a state, its citizens are still facing problems attributed to oil explorations and extractions; degradation of agricultural lands, mass displacement, and the widespread pollutions resulting in sufferings of local pastoralist and agricultural communities. In the case of oil pollution in South Sudan, "Unless coupled with a state industry commitment to the environment and to participatory space for affected communities, oil extraction has proven to be detrimental to neighboring communities and ecosystems" (Carmin & Agyeman, 2011).

Like many leaders in other developing countries, South Sudanese leaders will be more likely to collaborate with corporations in destructions of the environment and displacement of indigenous peoples. Nothing will be done in preventing destructions caused by the oil companies because "Many elites, profiting from the ongoing oil operations in one form or another, do not press to reduce pollution or clean up existing degraded sites for fear that the petroleum companies will reduce or eliminate the operations on which their own economic and social standing depend" (Carmin & Agyeman, 2011). This current pollution caused by oil production and extraction in the South Sudan will continue to head for the worst once numerous oil companies arrive in the country for explorations and extractions of the South Sudan's oil, unless its leaders will refuse to collaborate with oil companies, and will take a strong measure against oil companies by putting more restrictions regarding oil activities in the country.

THE FIGHT FOR THE CONTROL OF OIL

Border clashes regularly break out in oil-producing towns along the South and North-Sudan's border. These two sister states are trapped in a territorial dispute each claiming ownership of the oil–producing towns. In early April, 2012, South Sudanese army and the Sudanese army clashed over the control of oil town of Heglig (Panthou). In the process, Sudanese forces were defeated resulting in heavy losses; many human lives vanished including massive destructions of oil facilities and the whole town was burned into ashes. The South Sudanese forces occupied the town of Heglig for ten days before they withdrew due to condemnations and pressures from the international community. Out of anger and frustration, the Sudanese air force had been engaging in bombardments of the border towns and other territories inside the South Sudan. Many innocent civilians were killed, homes and properties were destroyed while thousands people have also fled the areas due to bombardments and artilleries attack from the Sudanese military.

This is reminiscent of Nigeria, where the ongoing conflict and instability is fueled by the Western corporations for control of the country's oil. The Niger Delta region has been the focus of the Western oil companies and the conflict concentrates in that region and slowly spreads to the rest of the country. The result of this conflict in Niger-Delta brought political and economic instability as well as environmental destructions in the country similar to ones that are occurring in South Sudan. Thus, "Oil companies are perpetrators in creating the region's woes" (Carmin & Agyeman, 2011). In the Niger-Delta, "The indigenous people have seen their home territories become host of more than 600 oil wells along with major oil transport and processing facilities, their overall living situation has decline in real terms" (Carmin & Agyeman, 2011). The displacements and environmental degradations are high in the Niger-Delta region. The "Pollution and environmental risk in Niger Delta have taken many forms, including land degradation from crude oil piping and refined product-tanker spills, gas flaring (largely of methane at the highest level of any refinery locations in the world" (Carmin & Agyeman, 2011). The "Spills from high-pressure pipelines and oil transfer annually numbered in the hundreds with perhaps 700,000 barrels escaping each year" (Carmin & Agyeman, 2011). For instance, "4835 spillage incidents were recorded (in the Delta) between 1976 and 1996-an average of 440 a year" (Carmin &Agyeman, 2011). These pollutions from spills have created severe health problems for the residents and their communities, whereas pollutions and environmental risks related to the ones in Nigeria contribute to the sufferings of people of the South Sudan as a result of oil extractions.

Similar practices instigated by the oil profiteers had taken place in Kenya in 2009 when the police carried out a campaign against indigenous Samburu pastoralist community causing death and displaced them from their homes to dry areas with no adequate water, causing even more suffering due to famine and disease. According to Huff & Philips, "The state violence against Kenyan indigenous pastoralists and Nigerian civilian in oil-rich regions has heightened, leaving thousands dead as militaries burn whole communities to the ground and police commit extrajudicial killings, rapes, beatings, thefts, arson, and intimidation" (2011). The related situation had happened in Nigeria as well when the military carried out helicopter and gunboat attacks on the civilians in the Delta-region, killing more than thousand people.

CHINESE INVOLVEMENTS IN AFRICA RESOURCES EXPLORATIONS AND TRADES

China is a rising global power and it is emerging politically and economically at amazing speed. This rising super power strives to control the world and to take over economic power from the United States over the next few years. While in the process of transition into economic power, it will commit many acts of destruction and atrocity similar to what most empires had committed over the years as they have been dictated by resources control to satisfy their greed. While China engages in various businesses in the global south nations and expands to the global north, incalculable abuses will also occur in those communities as a result of its operations as always a pattern for any empire.

The trade between China and Africa has increased dramatically in recent years with over an estimated of $56 billion in less than a half decade. China's imports from Africa mainly consist of oil and minerals. Specifically, "China has invested heavily in Sudan's oil exploration, chemical industry, and railway transport" (Bosshard, 2007). Likewise, in the last 7 years "Sudan provided 5% of China's oil imports, and it is the largest importer of Sudanese oil" (Bosshard, 2007). In particular, South Sudan is one of the countries rich in oil and other natural resources. "It is estimated that South Sudan sits on about 1% of world's oil reserves" (Bosshard, 2007). Since the discovery of its oil, there have been massive destructions of the environment and considerable health problems in communities attributing to oil explorations and extractions. These issues are mostly due to negligence or careless practices by Chinese's oil companies in their handling of oil wastes and extractions. This oil exploration and extraction in South Sudan reached its peak after the 2005 Comprehensive Peace Agreement (CPA) between the North-dominated government and the Sudan people Liberation Army (SPLA), and thereafter there has been substantial oil production and exploratory activities.

In general, "Research indicates that each step of the oil supply has potential to threaten the health of the communities and ecosystems" (Carmin & Agyeman, 2011). The activities such as drilling produces mud and effluents lead to contamination of water sources. These water sources in the areas of exploration extraction contain high amounts of concentration of chemicals, minerals, or mixed oil together with amount of contaminants such as chloride and hydrogen, well treatment chemicals, and oils which are very toxic. These pollute the surrounding areas in the Unity and the Upper Nile states in South Sudan. In Unity state, one NGOs employee who requested to remain unnamed due to fear of reprisal told journalists, "I witnessed oil workers dumping industrial waste into a nearby isolated pit in a dried swamp, which will flood in the rainy season and polluted the communities." He also added that, "I usually see men in aprons dig up huge pits and dump toxic wastes. They do not let anybody near that area" (Bar, 2009). Furthermore, there is a published report of fish being killed and vegetation being destroyed from direct release of toxic water that leaches directly into environment in the local rivers in South Sudan. German aid agency's vice-chairman, Klaus Stieglitz explains, "The chemical composition of water samples we have taken from oil well drilling pits is nearly the same as we found in the contaminated water boreholes the people are using for drinking water supply" (Bar, 2009). Stieglitz also added that, "The heavy metal concentrations in these waters will have negative impact on the health situation of the some 300,000 inhabitants of the affected area which covers 4,000 square kilometers (1,500 square miles)" (Bar, 2009).

Hence, oil exploration and extraction in the South Sudan's Unity and Upper Nile state is blamed for contaminating water which is spreading diseases to humans and cattle. It is feared that there could be environmental implications for the nearby Sudd swamp, one of the world's largest inland wetlands formed by the White Nile. Stieglitz also explains,

> The pollution caused by the oil industry is threatening the Sudd tropical wetlands, which cover an area of 30,000 square kilometers (11,500 square miles). The swamps, flood plains, and grasslands support a rich animal diversity including hundreds of thousands of migratory birds and are inhabited by the Nuer, one of southern Sudan's two main tribes. (Bar, 2009)

Additionally, survey released by the same German aid agency found that, "Oil exploration and exploitation in the oilfields of Mala and TharJath pose serious threats to human beings, livestock and the environment" (Bar, 2009). Another article from *South Sudan tribune* stated, "South Sudan villagers and environment suffers from oil boom" (Bar, 2009). In addition, one villager puts it, "Since water is contaminated, we have lost several cows and goats, said an elder from the Nuer ethnic group" (Bar, 2009).

This paragraph below explains the consequences of the oil exploration in South Sudan.

White Nile Petroleum Company (WNPOC), a consortium led by Malaysia's PETRONAS, in Unity State threatens the Sudd wetlands, the world's largest maze of swamps, lagoons and tributaries. Villagers accused oil companies for thousands of people who were forcefully evicted to make way for a low-sulphur crude oil venture in south-central Sudan. They say they lost venerated ancestral homes, died from contamination and saw livelihoods jeopardized. (Bar, 2009)

Furthermore, "German aid agency has accused an oil consortium in Southern Sudan of contaminating water supplies, affecting at least 300,000 people in Unity State" (Bar, 2009). "Since 2006, 27 adults and three children have died because of contaminated water from the oil field, said county commissioner in Koch, about 70 kilometers (44 miles) from Bentiu, the state capital. But more than 1,000 people are now sick with unknown illnesses" (Bar, 2009). The above statements are testimonies from local residents as well as aid workers who witnessed Chinese oil companies improperly dumping oil wastes and polluting oil producing regions (Unity and Upper Nile State).

Another study conducted by the United States Institute of Peace further finds that, "The oil industry exploited and polluted the area, wiping out the traditional livelihoods of fishing and farming" (Asuni, 2009). Thus, "Drilling, processing, and burning oil is dirty and damaging to the health of people everywhere, not to mention the health of the planet" (Leonard, 2010). As previously mentioned, these problems are currently happening in South Sudan as a result of oil exploration and extraction while government is not doing enough to stop or prevent these issues from happening.

THE UNITED STATES INVOLVEMENT IN AFRICAN OIL

The United States government had long been neglecting Africa's oil economy yielding it to China which is currently controlling half or almost the entire continent's resources. Due to the United States' increasing demands for energy consumption as a result of rapid population growth and corporation's desire of profit maximizations, the search for a new energy and other natural resources has solemnly intensified in recent years. "North-Africa and the Middle East produce nearly two-thirds of the oil in the world whereas North-Africa alone contains 7.2 percent of the world's confirmed reserves of oil-76.7 thousand million barrels more than the reserves of North America or former Soviet Union" (Perry &Wadhams, 2010). Therefore, United States desires to take total control of the continent's resources and enthusiastic to drive the Chinese oil companies out of Africa.

To secure African oil reserve, a lobby group for the oil industry (The African Oil Policy Initiative Group) has successfully lobbied and convinced the Bush administration to declare "The Gulf of Guinea in West Africa as an area of vital interest to America" (Barnes, 2005). These considerable investments bring increasing demands from corporations for military existence in the region, and recommended an establishment of a military subcommand for the Gulf of Guinea and other African countries known as African Command (AFRICOM). As stated, "The fight for access to world oil resources keeps on unabated resulting in some remarkable decisions originating from Washington and London" (Barnes, 2005). The paragraph below also provides summaries of its intentions.

> The U.S. involvement in Africa is growing following threats of terrorism and interruptions in oil production and because of the desires by foreign corporations to expand their activities on the continent. The response of American policymakers has been to set up a stronger military existence that will engage in counterterrorism programs and monitor oil installations. The objectives and degree of this increase and the principles legitimating it are not new. They are departures from Cold War policies. (Barnes, 2005)

This new unified regional U.S. Command for Africa (AFRICOM) was formed to expand the United States' interests in the regions with intention of protecting the United States' oil supplies in Africa and also to guarantee neoliberal policies while portraying this move as part of the war on terrorism with aim of preventing terrorist influence in the continent of

African. Noticeably, American government intervention in Third World in seeking the guarantee for oil sources is imposing negative effects on human rights, social justice, environment, and state formation. As Parenti explains, "Washington has supported some of the worst repressive regimes in the world; ones that regularly have indulged mass arrests, assassinations, torture, and intimidation" (1995).

Consequently, the thirst for oil and other natural resources that made the American government to keep ruthless leaders in power in Africa, Middle East, and the Latin America unveiled itself in the widespread social movements that have been sweeping North African and Middle Eastern countries starting in the spring of 2011 and beyond. Accordingly, "The oil-exporting countries exposed to a higher risk of uprising due to prolonged dictatorship leaders in power supported by the United States and the European nations" (Ikelebgbe, 2006). In the same way, "The response of American business leaders to weaknesses in the infrastructure and political order of African states (sic) has lead them to establish their own forms of community development, known as strategic philanthropy" (Barnes, 2005).

All these moves initiated by Washington pose severe negative consequences to those countries because they instigate internal conflicts between those who work for the interest of their citizens and the compradors class who desire to secure resources for themselves as well as for the foreign companies at the expense of the citizens of those nations. Equally, those problems previously mentioned had happened in the old Sudan before it split into two countries, hence, similar problems will also continue to take place in the South Sudan as long as foreign governments will have strong influence in the South Sudan's politic and economy. Likewise, several countries such as Gabon, Republic of Congo (Brazzaville), and Equatorial Guinea, Cameroon, Tunisia, Chad, and many others attracted the attention of the Western oil companies. They had civil wars or currently experiencing wars and environmental injustice fueled by the oil economy. So, various political economists believe that, "Developing countries with abundant natural resource tend to suffer from the "resources curses" and "double barreled" affliction of poor government and irresponsible economic behavior" (Ikelebgbe, 2006). Consequently, there have been more than 9 million refugees and internally displaced people because of conflicts fueled by oil and other natural resources and millions of people have been slaughtered from several conflicts and civil wars in Africa due to wars for the control of oil. Ikelegbe also point out that,

> From the time when the Cold War was in existence and the emergence of globalization, some nations or regions in Africa have not only fall shorted, but have also disintegrated into complete civil wars. The distinguished features of the civil strife in many of these states are conflicts over natural resources such as oil and diamonds. (2006)

CURRENT INTERNAL CHALLENGES IN NATION-BUILDING

High level of systemic corruption is another problem facing South Sudan and its citizens. It has been spreading like a wildfire all over the country. According to article on *http://www.sudantribune.com,* "Corruption is rife in South Sudan but no official has ever been prosecuted for graft since the SPLM gained power in 2005 as part of a peace deal with the north, which led to South Sudan's independence in 2011" (*2013*). This practice is widely carried out by dominant groups; the newly formed elite class, particularly those in leadership in all government institutions. It is becoming a widely practice and being carried out by everyone in the country. Likewise, there have been numerous allegations against several leaders in key positions taking bribes from the foreign corporations and businesses in order to secure ownership in companies. Some of these leaders are also accused of selling indigenous land. For instance, Eastern Equatoria state governor, Louis Lobong was "Accused of corrupt practices and illegal sale of lands to foreign investors in the state for self-benefit" (*http://www.sudantribune. com, 2012*). The Republic of the South Sudan is becoming the latest victims of the neoliberals' policy and the corporatocracy in collaboration with comprador class as it transitions into becoming a nation state. This is perhaps, the motives why the US, Britain, and other neighboring countries were supporting the political change in the old Sudan so that they are able to penetrate into South Sudan's economic system.

The foreign countries exploit the opportunity of creating the compradors class in the South Sudan as is always the pattern. "In many instances a comprador class emerged or was installed as a first condition for independence. Comprador class is one that cooperates in turning its own country into a client state for foreign interests" (Parenti, 1995). Those government officials who tend to engage in such activities do not have a clear understanding of what they are doing. They may not realize that they are betraying their own citizens by selling the country to foreign corporations; the country they fought for and liberated from former oppressors. Frank Fanon clearly described how comprador classes were established by neo-colonialism or neo-imperialism that plundered Algeria after its independence, as it is now the case in South Sudan.

> Spoiled children of yesterday's colonialism and today's governing powers oversee the looting of national resources and are ruthless in their scheming and legal pilfering. They use the poverty in nationwide to work their way to the top through import-export holdings, limited companies, playing the stock market, and nepotism. These spoiled leaders insist on the nationalization of business transactions, i.e., reserving contracts and business deals. Their doctrine is to claim the absolute need for nationalizing the theft of the nation. In this barren, nationalization phase, in this so-called period of austerity, their success at plundering the nation swiftly sparks anger and violence from the people. (Fanon, 2004)

The circumstance that had taken place in Algeria during the colonial period is reminiscent of what is happening in South Sudan; and it is jeopardizing the nation-building. Thus, South Sudan's economic dependency on foreign governments and corporations will severely restrain it from becoming a prosperous state. As Bond clearly states,

> Africa is poor, ultimately, because its economy and society have been ravaged by international capital as well as by the local elites who are often propped up by foreign powers. The public and private sectors have worked together to drain the continent of

resources which otherwise–if harnessed and share fairly–should meet the needs of the people of Africa. (2006)

The above paragraph is a clear illustration of what is occurring in South Sudan as the newly formed elites class awards contracts to foreign businesses in return of securing co-ownership of those businesses. As we speak, almost every government official in South Sudan is going through compradorization process; only very few are free from this practice.

Besides, Nepotism is widely practiced at all government levels. This practice evolves along tribal line and political party affiliations. It sabotages the development as well as the deliveries of services because qualified people are being prevented from filling positions that are relevant to their educations and qualifications just for a reason that they are either from other tribes or other political parties. For example, many branches of government institutions are being filled by unqualified relatives of persons in charge of institution. Others positions are allocated to invisible employees or best known as "Ghost Employees". Another problem that stand out is that salaries for employees in each department are given to those in charge of finance departments in their respective institutions because no electronic system in place where salary can be transferred directly into individuals' accounts. As a result, the finance officers in collaboration with their bosses usually choose which employee will get paid and who will not get paid each month by skipping those identified individuals. Additionally, each department is not interested in employing more people with intention to retain some positions for ghost employees. Bosses or departments' heads usually collect money that they intentionally allocate for those ghost employees and for those whose salaries are withhold for that month and use it for their personal needs, leaving many government employees with no incomes to feed their families for entire month or more. This illegal practice takes places due to lack of accountability and transparency within the government.

DOMINATION BY SPLM PARTY IN THE SOUTH SUDAN

The current ruling party, the Sudan People's Liberation Movement (SPLM) that composed of predominantly Dinka tribe and few from other tribes dominates the entire political arena in the South Sudan. The SPLM inherited this domination during the years of struggle. This single party's members control almost all government institutions and marginalizes other twenty two parties in newly founded nation. This imbalance of power among parties as well as among tribes creates divisions that have led to some groups to join the rebellions against the South Sudan government. The system of one party government has been proven to be disastrous because no check and balance in the government system and always leads to dictatorship and oppressive regimes. Thus, the SPLM party should allow other parties to participate in the political affairs in the country and they should share power with these parties because by just doing that will promote democracy, peace, and stability in this new nation.

TRIBAL DOMINATION AND CONFLICTS IN SOUTH SUDAN

Adding to many problems previously mentioned, the emerging tribal and class differentiation in South Sudan has become a serious problem facing the new nation as it has been a strategy by recolonizers to divide and conquer. Great resentments exist among all South Sudanese due to the domination by a few tribes or clans; particularly the ones that belong to the incumbent president Salva Kiir. People from Dinka tribe particular from Bhar-el-Ghazal region are known to occupy more ministerial positions in central government compared to the other tribes. They also dominate other positions in government institutions in this newly founded nation. This domination is believed to be the ongoing policy which initially emerged after the 1972 Peace Agreement when the South was granted regional autonomy by the Arab-dominated government in the North. For instance, "Throughout the late 1970s and early 1980s there were many Southerners who claimed the region was threatened by 'Dinka domination', the number of Dinka in regional government, in administration, and in some branches of security forces appear to them to be out of proportion to their qualification" (Johnson, 2003). In the current South Sudan government, the South Sudan Legislative Assembly is dominated by Dinka ethnic groups. Likewise, in recent appointment of the country's ambassadors and ministries, more than fifty percent of ambassadors and ministries appointed were from Dinka tribe, and only the remaining few positions are allocated to other 63 tribes. To justify this imbalanced representation, some people of Dinka tribe claim that they endured more suffering during years of struggle than the rest of the tribes. President Salva Kiir himself publicly spoke in one of his press conferences in Juba reconfirming this claim. He further restated that people from the Dinka tribe, particularly those from Bhar-el-Ghazal region, the area he comes from had gone through much suffering; therefore, they deserve to be allocated numerous government positions as rewards for their contributions and sufferings during the struggle against the North-dominated government. That was very unfortunate for the president of the country to address his people while endorsing tribalism in his speech.

Conversely, that claim is bogus because all tribes in South Sudan experienced almost similar sufferings and all fought in the war. Nuer tribe, for example, endured greater sufferings during the years of struggle because the Sudan People Liberation Army (SPLA) had their bases and headquarter in Nuer areas. The rebels used to depend on Nuers for food and other services. Whereas cattle or livestock that belong to Nuers were constantly slaughtered and rationed by the SPLA rebels. Nuer civilians were often caught up between the two movements, SPLA and Anya-nya-Two, and the SPLA used to accuse Nuer civilians of supporting Anya Anya-Two group. (Anya-nya-Two was rebel group predominantly made up of the Nuer tribe that fought against the SPLA due to conflict over the objective of the movement). As a result, large numbers of innocent civilians from Nuer lost their lives in cold blood or in conflicts when SPLA rebels attacked their villages. Their villages used to be destroyed by the same rebels. In addition, several Nuer young men were forcefully conscripted into rebel armies. The

Nuer men, women, young girls, and young boys were frequently forced to carry or transport rebels' ammunitions, rations, and heavy weapons during relocation or when launching attacks on government towns since rebels did not have vehicles available to transport their equipment during those years. Similar problems took place in Equatoria regions. Therefore, the president and the people from his tribe has no any reasons to marginalize others tribe on the pretext that they deserve to be awarded more seats and positions in the country that belong to all tribes.

Furthermore, the imbalanced tribal representation in the government of South Sudan as well as other issues led to the rebellions.

"In South Sudan's Jonglei State David Yauyau relaunched his rebellion earlier this year having signed a peace deal with the government in 2011. In Unity State, the South Sudan Liberation Army (SSLA) has fought the government since March 2011, despite some leading figures rejoining the government" (*http:// www.southsudan.net, September13, 2012*).

From the time of the referendum to present-day, there have been many clashes between the South Sudan government and the newly formed South Sudan rebel groups which are made up largely of Murlee, Nuer, Shilluk, and few Dinka ethnic groups from different states in South Sudan. Many lives have been lost from both sides, including civilians who are caught in cross fire between the two forces. Some civilians were intentionally attacked by the South Sudan government forces or newly formed rebels accusing them of supporting either government or rebels. As states, "The Waves of ethnic violences and rampant insecurity in its multiple forms across South Sudan still threaten the new nation's effort to achieve both economic and political stability" (*http://www.southsudan.net, 2012*).

The resentment attributable to tribal domination was echoed in the University of Juba campus, the main university in the country. I happened to be in the country when this incident took place and I was staying inside the University's staff compound with my cousin and family, professor, Lual Chany Chol who benevolently offers me an accommodation at his place while on the visit. After the deadly clash between the tribal groups, the Dinka tribe and the Equatorian tribes, the university was closed for six months. The clash was believed to be instigated by tribal and political motivations. Students as well as other members from Equatoria regions were angry at Dinkas on allegations that they (Dinkas) control everything from land to government in South Sudan. Equatorians accused Dinkas of land grabbing in Juba and in the whole greater Equatoria region. For that reason, people from this region as well as from other parts of the country see it unfair for one tribe, the Dinka in particular to marginalize other tribes in the newly founded nation while domination and marginalization were sole problems that led Southerners to take up arms and went to war against the people in the North. Therefore, many people in the South Sudan believe that people from the Dinka tribe are thriving while those from other tribes are slipping into deep poverty. Thus, this single tribe's domination being practiced in South Sudan is widely practiced in many other African countries which lead to serious internal conflicts among tribal groups as it is currently happening in South Sudan. This is also reminiscent of what took place in Rwanda which led to genocide in 1994.

In addition to tribal domination, tribal clashes caused by cattle rustling have threatened the peace and security in the newly founded nation. Several ethnic groups such as Murlee, Nuer, and Dinka tribes engage in these activities. Youths from these ethnic groups who have no other means of earning incomes tend to steal cattle belong to other ethnic groups in order to sell them for money, use them to pay dowries, or keep them as source of wealth. These civilians have armed themselves with weapons such as RPG's, AK-47's, and other machine guns. They unlawfully use these weapons in raiding other's villages and in cattle rustling. As a result, thousands of civilians' lives vanish due to the ongoing cattle rustling conflicts. These conflicts can easily shift into a major tribal war in the country if not resolved. The South Sudan government has been trying to disarm these civilians but is unsuccessful because the government in North Sudan is still trying to undermine the new South Sudan government. The Sudan government resupplies and funds civilians and other rebel groups that operate in South Sudan in order to create bigger insecurity in the newly formed nation. Aras explains, "The Sudan People's Liberation Movement claims to have evidence that Khartoum supplied southern rebels with weapons, so as to enable them to remove the new southern government from power before the official declaration of independence"

(2011). Similarly, South Sudanese people had lived under oppression and chaos for over four decades. They have been traumatized and still suffer as a result of past experiences making them grasp violent rather than peace. Thus, it becomes the best interest of their former oppressor to continue keeping them in the same state of chaos.

To relate what is happening in South Sudan to Frank Fanon's analysis during the Algerian conflict against the West's domination, "The colonists keep the colonized in a state of rage which make the colonized caught up in the knit web of colonialism where the buildup tensions of those colonized periodically erupts into the bloody fighting between tribes, clans, or individuals" (Fanon, 2004). For the sake of peace, development, and avoidance of genocide, South Sudanese leaders and their civilians should merely engage in activities that promote peace, unity, development, and the eradication of illiteracy rather than fighting among themselves. Thus, these problems together with other related issues are creating widespread mistrust and animosity among South Sudanese citizens that can easily burst into major conflict on tribal line in the country.

MY TRIP TO SOUTH SUDAN AFTER THE INDEPENDENCE

My original plan was to witness the historical independence of my country of origin on July 9, 2011; however, I was in Australia on a visit to reunite with some of my relatives whom I had been separated for more than twenty-five years as a result of the civil war. So, I returned to South Sudan precisely six months after the country gained its independence. It was my second visit since I left the country in 1987, and my first visit to Juba, the capital of South Sudan. Once I was in South Sudan, my experiences were mix of happiness and sadness. I was thrilled to see my fellow country men and women finally free and live in high spirits in their own nation. I was also mesmerized to see South Sudanese natives occupied all top government positions; the positions used to be occupied by people from the north Sudan prior to the split. Almost all South Sudanese government officials were driving expensive cars; each estimated over one hundred thousand dollars, the kinds of cars were usually driven by the Northern brothers and sisters before South separated from the North. I could not help but shared excitement even though I was unhappy with new elites who enriched themselves by pilfering oil revenues and donors' money that could have been used for development and for providing social services for the people. I was also outraged to see average citizens in the country still struggle due to inability of the government, and its newly corrupted officials to provide services to the people because the money supposedly allocated for social services and for salaries of new hired government employees usually distribute by bosses through what so called services and allowances for housing, cars, food, and other services including entertainments and vacationing. The practice is saddened because such money could be use to feed poor people who go to bed hungry in many towns and villages everywhere in the country.

RACE TO BECOME MILLIONAIRES IN THE REPUBLIC OF SOUTH SUDAN

In additional to various problems previously mentioned a widespread craving to become a millionaire in the South Sudan is an issue that threats the new nation's prosperity. The race started immediately after the signing of the Comprehensive Peace Agreement (CPA) in 2005. It continued through the transition period, and carried on well after the independence. This marathon of becoming a millionaire embarked on with money donated by international communities with the intent of helping the South Sudanese civilians who were in desperate need, and to revitalize the region that has been devastated by decades of war. Instead of reaching the desperate people and to use it in services delivery, and to rebuilding the country, these donations fell into the hands of corrupt officials. These individuals have no vision of building this new nation instead they accumulate wealth for self-enrichments at the expenses of ordinary people who are left dying of hunger and curable diseases. These corrupt officials are only concern more of becoming elites in the newly founded nation, making them to become obstacles to development. In the process, most government officials in every branch of South Sudan government have pocketed this donated money as much as possible and diverted it into their private accounts in foreign countries. They used this money to send their families to foreign countries, bought big houses and expensive cars for their families, and put their children into the best schools in many foreign countries (Kenya, Ethiopia, Uganda, United States, and Australia just to mention a few). The same individuals continue craving to embezzle more so that each become among the first group of millionaires in a country where "73% of men and 84% of women are illiterate; 4.7 million of its 8 million populations are food insecure; 50% of its civil servants are estimated to lack the appropriate qualifications and 87% of the population lack access to basic health care" (*www.Sudan tribune.net, 2012*).

Additionally, there was reported 2 billion dollars worth of grains and more than 4 billion dollars disappeared and unaccountable for. Nobody knows where this money went and no one is brought to justice or at least can explain what has happened to this money. Thus, the South Sudan government has been warned numerous times by the international communities such as United Nations and the United States, the main donors to South Sudan to refrain from corruption and hold accountable individuals who took part in the corruption activities and called for their dismissal from the government offices, however, nothing has been done because the corruption is being practiced administratively and most government officials involve either in a small or larger scale.

Likewise, at the end of the transition period, there has been a great influx of foreigners as well as South Sudan natives from Diasporas whose aim was to rob the new country and its people. As clearly stated,

In the run-up to its anticipated inauguration as a new capital, Juba has become a boomtown, drawing a motley crew of chancers: logistics experts, car salesmen, development workers, and working girls. But an economy in which the big money—from aid and oil—goes to foreign contractor or foreign bank accounts held by southern-Sudanese officials leaves most ordinary people basing their hopes for future prosperity on the wallets of a few thousand foreigners" (Aras, 2011).

Hence, it becomes obvious that individualism has taken over our societies and weakened our co-existences. Therefore, in South Sudan in particular, everyone is pursuing self-enrichment rather than collective interests. So, it is widely understood in South Sudan that an individual's success takes precedent over public success in term of material wealth. On the contrary, long before the independence, South Sudanese used to share and care for each other even during the war when resources were scarce but now the long practiced culture totally vanished. This culture of selfishness has never been a South Sudanese culture; perhaps, this is because many Southerners have lost touch with the real South Sudanese culture due to many years of living in war, in refugee's camps, or in foreign countries, and not to mention the adaptation of foreign cultures imposed on them while in those foreign countries. It is unfortunate for self-enrichment to become a sub culture which is beginning to override the main culture in South Sudan.

Another speculation is that when SPLA rebels (now South Sudan government officials) were in the bush fighting against the Khartoum regime, they had never had opportunity of accumulating wealth; therefore, they ought to exploit this opportunity in the existing weak system to accumulate millions of dollars in a very short period of time without being held accountable for embezzlement. They assumed that they are entitled to rob the country off its resources since they fought for it; the government has turned a blind eye on those individuals that abuse public fund for personal gains. This practice makes many people to wonder why those South Sudanese officials are opting self-enrichment and elitism rather than building the nation since there are lack of developments and delivery of services in this country where millions of citizen are going to bed hungry, thousands are still dying from curable diseases, and the illiteracy rate is hovering over seventy percent. Yet, those government officials desperately want to get rich quick at the expense of the general population.

Furthermore, during my three months stay in the capital, Juba, I walked on foot and rode in public transportation to every corner of the city to have a clear understanding of what was taking place in my native country. Surprisingly, I saw numerous high rise buildings with more than two-story high which contain five or more bedrooms that belong to those who work in the government. Those big houses could not be built with small salaries that one earned only in six months or less on the job. The question one could ask, where do these people get such a huge amount of money from in just a short period of time on the job with salary under ten thousand dollars a year? The answer is surely corruption. Not to mention that one of my close relatives once jokingly told me when I inquired that, "South Sudanese are corrupted from office cleaners all the way to the top office in the country". Indisputably, after spending more time in the country, I had to agree with his statement once I personally witnessed what was happening.

Hence, in an attempt to curb this corruption practice, "The country's vice president, Riek Machar has called on the international community to the nation to help build its institutions and instill effective systems of accountability and transparency to tackle the corruption problem" (*http://www.southsudan.net, 2012*). Also, President Salva Kiir pleads to the identified 75 officials responsible for more than two billion dollars that has vanished in South Sudan and requested that this money should be returned, yet no single official response to his request.

To enhance the call for ending the corruption, South Sudanese must institute a favorable culture where collective interest takes precedent over individual interest. As Smith argues that, "Our tendency towards self-love is controlled by our capacity sympathetically to identify with emotional states of others: And hence it is, that to feel much for others and little for ourselves, that restrain our selfish, and to indulge our benevolent affections, constitutes the perfection of human nature" (Callincos, 1999). This is what the people of South Sudan must embrace to change their current mindsets in order to tackle some of these problems that are caused by greed. David Gressly, the U.N.'s regional coordinator in Juba, also clearly understood when he mentioned that, "It will take a generation before Southern Sudan is fully formed. "Real success will take 20 to 25 years" (Aras, 2011).

INFLUX OF FOREIGN CITIZENS AND INVESTORS INTO SOUTH SUDAN

Moreover, during my brief stay in South Sudan, I was surprised by the large number of foreigners who were endlessly arriving in the country. This influx began after the signing of the Comprehensive Peace Agreement in 2005 when business-minded individuals or entrepreneurs from Somalia, Ethiopia, Kenya, Uganda, and other countries rushed into South Sudan to start up businesses. Others from the same countries went to South Sudan in order to look for employment opportunities from NGOs that operate in the country. Some have also decided to move into South Sudan to start a new life. As the number of foreigners increase, sentiments toward these foreigners greatly increased. Ordinary citizens fear that their country is infiltrated by foreigners and that they are taking jobs away from them as it is generally a case in different countries. Their claims become entirely true because most of the NGOs jobs occupied and run by the foreigners. Even some of the jobs in the government of South Sudan are also occupied by foreigners leaving many South Sudanese citizens with no or fewer jobs to occupy. From out of concerns and observation, I anticipate that this massive influx of foreigners will impose negative consequences on the nation's affairs in coming years because South Sudan economy will be dominated by citizens from bordering states and that will make foreign citizens to have immense influences in the government decision-making process and will eventually manipulate the South Sudan political matters. These foreigners also involve in all businesses in the country ranging from hotels to retail shops, and they mostly employ only people from their native countries while local nationals are being left unemployed and also pushing out the South Sudanese who might have small capital to start up business. Their present in the country will also create additional problem in the years down the road because they are draining the resources as well as expatriating profits to their native countries rather than to spend portions of their profits on South Sudan development. As it is mentioned that, "Investors go into a country not to uplift it but to enrich themselves" (Parenti, 1995). These problems must be addressed by the government itself because there are enough qualified South Sudanese that can be employed by those NGOs but are now wandering in streets in every city in South Sudan with no jobs opportunities in reach. Besides, South Sudan citizens who are willing to start up small businesses are being blocked by these foreigners. They are being driven out of business opportunities due to limited capitals or resources to compete with businesses owned by foreigners with abundance capitals.

LACK OF FREEDOM AND EQUALITY IN SOUTH SUDAN

There are many reported violations of human rights and freedom of speech throughout the South Sudan. Local journalists are being detained for speaking out or expressing their concerns. Leaders of other political parties are also being detained for criticizing the ruling party's policies, and for demanding more political representation in the government. The United States ambassador to South Sudan, Susan Page warned that, "Democracy is hard earned, but lost easily" (*http://www.sudantribune.com, 2012*). She further stated that, "It is easy to become impatient with the pace of change and imperfect democratic processes, and want to force that change along by undemocratic means" (*2012*). The United States ambassador to South Sudan was cautioning South Sudan leaders on the slow implementation of democracy after South Sudanese voted overwhelmingly in the referendum through democratic process that led to the independence of the South Sudan. During the post-independence thus the same leaders who embraced the democratic process are now working against it.

These leaders need to allow citizens or the civil society to express their views or concerns openly without being apprehended by the government security's agents so that they are aware of public outcry concerning problems facing the citizens. As Hegel argues,

When the activity of civil society is restricted, it is occupied internally with expanding its population and industries'. As a result, 'the accumulation of wealth increases…but on the other hand, the specialization and limitation of particular work also increase, as do likewise the dependence and want of class which is tied to such work; this in turn leads to inability to feel and enjoy the wider freedoms, and particularly the spiritual advantages, of civil society. (Callinicos, 1999)

I regard to gender equality, women are earnestly underrepresented in the South Sudan government. They are only allocated twenty-five percent representations in the government. However, this policy is not fully implemented because only few women hold ministerial positions in the current government either in the central or in the state government. Perhaps, the number of women holding top government positions will increase once gender equality law is created and implemented in the South Sudan, and when more women become better educated. Presently, government claims that there are no enough qualified and well educated women in the country, whereas this claim is just an excuse for patriarchy and sexism.

Furthermore, there is no law that protects women from spousal abuse. Children are not protected from parental abuse as well. For instance, during my trip in South Sudan, one evening I heard a helpless and desperate voice of a young boy probably between ten and twelve years old being beaten by his father two blocks away from my parents' home. A beating that lasted more than five minutes and I could hear the boy pleading for help. I wanted to go to their place in order to convince his father to stop beating the boy, but my father would not allow me to interfere because according to the culture in that part of the world, a child or a wife is still being punished by beating as a part of disciplinary action if one partakes in wrongdoing. The culture that is so backward and detrimental, it must be renounced. Coming from a Social Responsibility background, I was completely outraged by the horrible beating. I wanted to go to their residence and help the young boy but I failed to do so because I had to take heed of my father's advice, who warned me not to get involved. He advised me that I must respect the local culture while I was staying with them in the town. I became very disturbed by it and wished for the government to create the laws that prevent children and women from horrific treatments. At this time, South Sudan is in a transitional period. Perhaps, in the next few years government will create laws to protect women and children from spousal and parental abuses. Let us be hopeful that the government put the system in place sooner so that innocent children and women do not have to go through these kinds of abuses any longer.

FORCED MARRIAGE IN SOUTH SUDAN

Forced married still exists in South Sudan. Parents forced their daughters to marry those are not their daughters' choices just for the sake of families' economic security. Parents also force their daughters to marry at a very young age. According to article on *https://www.hrw.org/news*, "Girls in South Sudan told Human Rights Watch that family members forced them to marry in exchange for dowry payments. Girls who try to resist forced marriages suffer brutal consequences at the hands of their families" (2013). Also, from government statistics, "Close to half of South Sudanese girls between 15 and 19 are married, with some marrying as young as age 12" (*https://www.hrw.org/news, 2013*). Below are some of the reasons of why early marriage is still widely practiced in South Sudan.

> Early marriage is a deeply-rooted cultural practice common amongst the Nuer and Dinka ethnic groups. They also claimed that the pride and financial gain involved in receiving marriage-wealth in the form of cattle is a significant contributing factor for some parents. The focus upon wealth can also lead young girls to marry men much older than them. It is common practise for girls between the ages of 15 and 17 to marry, despite the legal age being 18. (*http://www.sudantribune.com, 2012*)

Similarly, "Child marriage frequently interrupts girls' education—or deprives them of it altogether" (Sic) and "The country's widespread child marriage exacerbates South Sudan's pronounced gender gaps in school enrollment, contributes to soaring maternal mortality rates" (*https://www. hrw.org/news,2013*). Consequently,

Child marriage also puts girls at greater risk of death or ill-health because of early pregnancy and childbirth. Reproductive health studies show that young women face greater risks in pregnancy and child birth than older women, including life-threatening obstructed labour due to their smaller pelvises and immature bodies – problems accentuated by South Sudan's limited prenatal and postnatal healthcare services. (*https://www.hrw.org/news, 2013*)

ANIMALS JUSTICE IN SUDAN

In addition, South Sudan has no effective law that protects animals or wildlife. Animals are being treated inhumanely, and killed for no apparent reason. For example, tame animals such as dogs and cats are being killed daily on streets or at residences by individuals or owners. Other wild animals are widely hunted for food and for other purposes. For instance, elephants, leopards, or tigers are targeted for their ivories and their skins by South Sudan citizens and by foreign businesses. The minister of wildlife has not yet enforced strict rules and regulations that protect animals and other wildlife. Perhaps, in the coming years the government will create and implement strong law that will protect South Sudan's wildlife.

INFLUX OF RETURNEES FROM DIASPORAS AND THEIR REJECTION IN SOUTH SUDAN

After South Sudan gained its independence, large numbers of South Sudanese who had been displaced by war enthusiastically returned home in order to take part in nation-building. However, these returnees were received with resentment by people who remained in the country during the war. The returnees are faced with feelings of what psychologists called "Attitudinal rejection". People who remained in the country during the war perceive the returnees from Diasporas as threats. They see them as having better educations and more qualifications. Thus, they fear that the returnees will take their jobs away from them. Therefore, this resentment shapes the way the returnees are received by people who work in the government. It is becoming more difficult for the returnees to be employed in government institutions and penetrate into the system that has been established by their counterparts who mostly have less qualification. Some people in the government also fear that those who come from Diasporas will change the high level of systemic corruption and nepotism being practiced in all government levels. It becomes a war-like situation between the South Sudanese from Diasporas and those who remained in the country during the war.

Consequently, South Sudanese leaders need to learn from history about why South Sudan was marginalized by the North Sudan. The marginalization was in fact due to the lack of educated Southerners during the earlier years of independence. The Arabs in the North took advantage of it since there were no well educated Southerners who worked in the government before and after Sudan gained its independence. The Arabs descents had upper hands in education which enabled them to marginalize the Africans in the South resulting in civil war that lasted for four decades. The current resentment from those in the government toward people returning from Diasporas is polarizing the country and it is creating unintended consequences. It will also have a boomerang effect sooner or later because people with better education and more qualifications are being blocked from working in the government. In the end, many South Sudanese from Diasporas will return to their adapted country abroad while the ones with less education and qualifications remain to run the government affairs and other services which will result in weak and poor system in place.

Thus, people with different experiences and education from the West and others African countries should be incorporated in the government in South Sudan so that they would be able to contribute positively in the nation-building. As one Somali-American professor, Ahmed Samatar pointed out, "People from the Diasporas are thought to have better education, better access, and better understanding of the world system, and maybe that's one way they have better credibility within the country" (*http://minnesota.publicradio.org, 2012*). The professor was referring to his return to Somalia after 35 years in the United States in order to take part in his native country's nation- building similar to what many South Sudanese are intending to do.

Likewise, the returnees are blamed for fleeing and not taking part in the war. Nonetheless, in reality, South Sudanese from Diasporas have significantly contributed to ending the conflict. Some of them were also prior military personnel and veterans of the Sudan People Liberation Army (SPLA). Many of them carry wounds from the war. Others live with permanent disabilities they sustained in battles against the North. Not to mentioned that South Sudanese in Diasporas, particularly those who live in North America (USA and Canada), Europe, and Australia have made huge contributions in term of human capitals as well as in social empowerments in South Sudan. These individuals sponsored a high number of South Sudanese sons and daughters at schools both in the North Sudan and neighboring countries during the war. They continue to carry on this duty until now, even after the independence. Some of the South Sudanese who had been sponsored by those living in the West are currently working in many institutions in South Sudan, and they are making positive contributions as well.

Also, the same South Sudanese in the Western World have contributed to the livelihoods of many Southerners by sending money to their friends and relatives in refugee's camps in neighboring countries and in South Sudan as well. They also used to contribute money to be used in renting offices and houses for the SPLAs rebels and their families in neighboring countries such as Kenya, Ethiopia, and Uganda. They used to send money to buy military gears and communication equipment (Satellite phones, video cameras, etc.).

I must truly proclaim that any Southern Sudanese who had lived or still live in Diasporas have contributed tremendously to bring the Sudan conflict to an end. I can also attest that South Sudanese who went to school in Western countries at some point have written college papers about Sudanese conflict as part of their school-works and presented them to their colleagues and professors as elements of the awareness. They have also brought awareness at their work places, churches, or in other settings. The South Sudanese in Diasporas have significantly contributed in bringing the current peace in Sudan by bringing awareness to international communities, and made the conflict broadly known to the rest of the world. Without the

South Sudanese that live in the Diasporas, the Sudanese problem could not be understood by the international community. Hence, people in Diasporas are among those who made the independence of the Republic of South Sudan possible. Now in return, they are being blocked from taking part in the nation's building and turned away forcing many of them to return to their adopted countries in the West.

Additionally, during the referendum, almost all South Sudanese in the United States had to drive for more than 8 hours to Voting Centers to register and vote in the referendum. They stood in line outside for more than twelve hours in the shivering winter cold with snow falling down on them for the sake of casting their votes in the country's historical referendum. I personally witnessed it when people passed out due to severe winter cold while standing in lines at the polling stations outside and had to be rushed to hospital. Through determination and commitment to South Sudan, I and many other Southerners were able to caste our vote and played a big role in bringing the independence.

Equally, being one among many South Sudanese who yearn to take part in the nation-building, my ambition compelled me to abandon a comfortable life-style in the United States where I had left behind a nice car, air conditioned house/apartment, good security, and many other good things for the sake of taking part in the nation-building. I walked on foot in a sweltering heat in the city of Juba and slept in poor ventilated rooms just for a chance to contribute in building the new nation. I consider it an enormous sacrifice because after growing up in the United States and living comfortably for almost twenty years, once must confess that it is indeed a sacrifice to return to South Sudan and start a new life all over again. Likewise, being a South Sudanese by birth as well as having parents, siblings, and relatives in South Sudan, I remained connected with them and share their grievances and happiness. Accordingly, I had to return to South Sudan and tried to either volunteer or to acquire employment in various institutions where I could contribute positively and help in bringing change collectively with those who had made similar decision. Nevertheless, I was constantly turned away.

From a discouragement and exhaustion going from one office to another, and contacting individuals who might be willing to offer me a possibility though nobody paid attention because everyone was busy devising next a strategy to embezzle; I ultimately decided that I had given it the benefit of the doubt, and I had walked passably in that sweltering heat on the street of Juba, thus, I returned to the United States where I called it a home for the last twenty years; a country that offered me many opportunities specifically the education, and helped me to redefine who I am today. Frankly speaking, I am better off to live in the United States because I have established myself here and I have achieved scores of positive things that could never be possible anywhere and I continue to excel.

CONCLUSION

It is doubtful that there will ever be permanent peace and stability as well as social and environmental justice in Africa. The continent is vulnerable to resources expropriations and land grabbing by capitalist countries. Andrzejewski explains, "To increase their wealth, individuals, groups, nations, and corporation have travelled to the globe for thousands of years expropriating land and natural resources that did not belong to them, and exploiting the labor of people and animals" (2009). The same capitalist countries together with transnational corporations have tendency to fuel conflicts, set off wars, political turmoil, and economics instability in global South nations. In addition, wars instigated by these capitalist countries and transnational corporations cause vast social problem that affects everyone in numerous countries. They disrupt the livelihood of the people, destroy social systems, kill innocent people, and force others to migrate to different countries. Not to mention that transnational corporations influence powerful governments such as the United States and others to carryout wars on their behalf. Thus, African governments become susceptible to the influences of foreign corporations and their governments making it even more difficult to thwart corporations from exploration and extraction of resources, improper disposal of toxic chemicals from oil, mining, and other hazardous wastes. It is also apparent that economic and political systems in countries that engage in war are at risk and habitually collapse due to the resources being drained or channeled into military to acquire military equipment where foreign corporations and imperialists government benefits. As a result, limited resources or no resources are left to provide for citizens such as food, healthcare, jobs, and other essential needs. This was a case in the Sudan and also in other African countries. Klein explains, "The primary economic role of wars, however, was as a means to open new markets that had been sealed off and to generate postwar peacetime booms" (2007). So, it becomes clear that the economic role of wars divulges itself in South Sudan where various foreign businesses have relocated to South Sudan in the post-civil war era. These foreign businesses are now reaping fruits of South Sudanese's struggle while citizens of this new state continue to live in misery.

Therefore, citizens of developing nations must continue to advocate against foreign governments to stop funding wars. If necessary, they must continue lobbying their own governments in order to persuade them not to work for the interests of foreign corporations. In addition, unless industrialized nations find alternative sources of energy that impose less threat to environment, peace, and stability in Africa and in the rest of the world, the indigenous people, animals, and environment will continue to pay the price.

Besides, nations or world leaders need to resolve conflicts and other issues through diplomatic means rather than through military means. Utilizing force and violence as means to resolve conflicts is proven to be not effective for real peace; it is only effective for the continued theft of resources and for corporation to make huge profits. Many nations tried this approach overtime and it has never been a practical solution. The world experienced it in Vietnam, Iraq, Afghanistan, Sudan, and others countries around the globe and yet nothing good is being accomplished other than complete destructions in those countries.

Furthermore, capitalism is a system of taking more and leaving nothing for the rest. This system is proven to create a society of selfishness and individualistic; and it also enhances environmental inequality and racism by polluting communities in the developing countries while imposing severe risk on people, the environment, and animals. So, the capitalist is preoccupied with desire to make hug profit with no regard of consequences. Parenti states, "Capitalist ceaselessly searches for ways of making more money in order to make still more money" (1995).

Similarly, capitalists are guided by a false belief that since the destruction they create does not happen in their back yard, it is not a threat to them; however, their actions are coming back to haunt them regardless of distance since the world is now interconnected through globalization and technology. Hence, there will always be boomerang-effects because contaminated foods produced in global South nations will also make their way into capitalist countries.

Additionally, with China moving toward capitalism and a rising empire, it will engage in unfair trade with many countries. It will continue to commit human rights violations and environmental destruction. Therefore, through regulation and cutting back on consumption and overexploitation of resources, there could be less pollution and related problems in the South Sudan as well as in the rest of the world. Above and beyond, human must change the way it does thing to save the world from destruction.

Moreover, oil companies from China and the West compete for the control of oil in South Sudan making it a battleground for resource grabbing and can eventually lead to civil war. The oil extraction and exploration will continue to pose problems in South Sudan while the government is still in transitional phase with no regulations in place. Despite that NGOs strive to discourage oil companies from polluting the environment, persuading them to adhere to international environmental regulations, carrying out independent research and investigate the ongoing health issues and environmental problems in South Sudanese communities affected by pollution due to oil operations, and raising pollution matters, and present their findings to the Republic of South Sudan government in expectation of establishing regulations against oil companies to reduce pollution problems in oil producing states, yet the NGOs are unsuccessful in their attempts. Therefore, it will take South Sudan government several years to create strong and effective system that hold oil companies accountable for environmental pollutions that is now imposing health problems and threatening the region's ecosystem.

Historically, a country must have educated sons and daughters in order to have better development and good governance or a better system of all kinds. If educated South Sudanese from Diasporas are not given opportunities to take part and work in the government institutions, then, these people will abandon the country and return to their respective adopted countries, yielding the country to the less educated to run the government. Hence, the problem that faces people from Diasporas in South Sudan must be addressed. The returnees must be recruited and employed in the South Sudan government so that there are effective government systems run by well qualified and educated citizens. Otherwise, massive brain-drains will arise in South Sudan sooner than later if the government of South Sudan and its leaders do not change their attitude toward these returnees.

Also, President Salva Kiir needs to discontinue issuing decrees and refrains from other related practices that promote corruption, nepotism, disunity, and conflict in the new nation. Salva Kiir and his team should only devote more time and resources for common goals such as development, peace, unity, equality, freedom, and stability in the country. Imperatively, the most significant thing for any leader to do if he or she loves his or her country is to devote his or her time to provide services and to care for his or her people. President Salva Kiir and his team thus must follow the same principal in order to be a true leader that serves the interest of his people.

Citizens must also continue to advocate for freedom and justice in the South Sudan. Unless the government begins to recognize the need of citizens' involvement in the decision-making process and allow them to determine the future of this country as they did in the referendum in January, 2011, otherwise, South Sudan will have many years ahead before achieving a true democracy, and it will probably be included among countries which violate the rights of their citizens.

The leaders of the Republic of South Sudan must be watchful of transnational corporations and neo-liberal policies in order to protect the country and its civilians, animals, the land, and resources from destruction and expropriation. They must fight against corporations to cease land-grabbing and resource exploitation together with other leaders of the global South nations.

While the need for profitability and the ambitions of economic and political elites from time to time take precedent over the social and environmental concerns, there must be a serious need for "Protocols that ensure transparency and procedures that will hold corporations and government accountable for their actions" (Carmin & Agyeman, 2011). Likewise, corporate influence and western imperialism together with the lack of focus from the South Sudan government may lead one to foresee numerous problems in South Sudan that will affect the people, environment, and other species. I hope that corporations as well as neo-liberal's policies will not instigate conflict in the South Sudan. This country has been already ravaged by many decades of war, and I expect for this new country to have a permanent peace and to become a prosperous state.

Lastly, after I studied in Social Responsibility program it has enabled me to view individual problems and social problems from sociological imagination. It also helped me to understand obstacles that prevent individuals or leaders from solving or ameliorating problems facing the people or the society; among these obstacles are power, legitimating, vested interest, and other factors. So, in order to solve social problems thus people must first identify the root causes and attempt to eliminate it if possible so that they would be able to solve other social problems since most problems are interconnected. South Sudanese must also tackle their social issues by employing different sociological approaches such as radical sociology, liberation sociology, and public sociology which these approaches empower and mobilize citizens to address social issues. People must also continue to fight for social justice and equality because there is no absolute justice in every society since justice is defined in many ways by different people as laws are created to protect the rich and powerful. As I acquired much knowledge in various issues which some of them are mentioned in this book, I begin to ask myself what I would do if I happened to be in a top leadership position in South Sudan or elsewhere? Could I still be a leader for positive change? Would I follow the evil deeds of other leaders or should I choose a path different from those leaders who are infamous for killing and for destructions either in their own countries or in other nations? These questions are left unanswered until the day I will be in a top leadership position so that I weigh what I have learned in the Social Responsibility program against the reality of evil or good leaders. Thus, in looking at my past and the country I originated from, I must admit that I am blessed and fortunate to be alive today after going through difficulties throughout my childhood. Of course, I give thank to the God for guaranteeing my health and keeping me safe. I am also privileged to reach at Master's degree level and successfully attained this educational goal after many years of hardship. Something that I was only dreaming of it many years back as it was dictated by lack of opportunity. I am exceptionally humbled by this struggle because I know that there are many other South Sudanese who have tried to achieve their education but they have never had the opportunity to make this dream come true.

ACTION PLANS AND RECOMMENDATIONS FOR SOUTH SUDAN

Once: Currently, there is no accountability and transference in the country. Those who habitually involve in corruption are practicing it freely without being charge for wrong doings. There is an urgent need for laws and regulations for accountability. Officials who divert public money for private uses should not only be relieved from their positions but must be sent to prison and banned from working in any government institutions upon their release. The money must be recouped and their properties must be confiscated and sold with proceeds going toward the repayment of stolen public money.

Two: Since multiple political parties and tribes are not equally represented in political structure in South Sudan, the SPLM party needs to change its ideology and relinquish some key positions to other parties that are underrepresented in order to have political stability. There must be equal representation in government's ministerial positions or top positions, perhaps distributed equally among tribes base on regional location or states. Besides, top government positions can be assigned to only qualify candidates with strong educational backgrounds in their respective positions. The President should also refrain from appointing government officials by decrees. In many cases, party members hand-pick unqualified individuals from their own parties, tribes, or clans and that initiate division and mistrust among the people. Since those being appointed for positions do not remain on the job long enough, these individuals embezzle much money as they can for duration on the job because they anticipate that their removable are imminent. These kinds of practices are fueling corruption.

Three: In order to promote public health in South Sudan, government must dramatically improve the quality of drinking water. It must also regulate oil operations more rigorously. Devise clean up strategies, introduce corporate social responsibility, and enlist the support of oil producers states in the country as well as major state governments, international organization, and NGOs because "In a globalized world, environmental problems are framed global problems with global solution" (Carmin &

Agyeman, 2011). Similarly, "With globalized investment and production and several pressing transnational environmental effects of human activity, the transnational networks of NGOs, international institutions, and the interaction of the two have become crucial resources for strengthening local voice and power" (Carmin & Agyeman, 2011). Thus, the South Sudan government and its citizens must demand more strict ethical rules from companies from China, the United States, and other industrialized nations and it must require them to abide by the South Sudanese government's laws and regulations and follow proper practices if they want to operate in the South Sudan.

Fourth: South Sudan government must also recognize the need for educated and qualified people in the government. It must incorporate South Sudanese from Diasporas who may possess more education and qualifications instead of perceiving them as threats. By doing just that it will help the country to move forward because these individuals are able to introduce fresh ideas and also bring different expertise that can be incorporated into the government's functional system.

Fifth: Child protection and spouse protection laws must be created so that children and women can live in a society that guarantees them freedom from any harm. South Sudan government must also take the issue of illiteracy seriously and makes education a priority. This education must be encouraged and must be provided free for all. Government must build more schools in every county while providing qualified teachers and free transportation for these children. In the next twenty years or so, the country should have a high percentage of people who know how to read and write so that the South Sudan work force has more skilled and qualified workers.

Sixth: Underage or forced marriages must be discouraged by creating laws that ban this practice. This practice puts young girls at risk during pregnancy and at child birth. It also prevents them from pursuing their educations and it destroys their dreams. Animal protection laws need to be created. Animals must be allowed to live freely in their natural habitat free from human interference such as pouching and bondage.

Seventh: South Sudan leaders must not allow privatization and deregulation to take shape in the country because it will only jeopardize the delivery of services and enable western governments and corporations to hijack state's owned enterprises and natural resources. It should avoid borrowing heavily from the World Bank and the IMF because the country has enough wealth that can bring sufficient revenues for use in feeding its people as well as for development and other services.

Eighth: Social services similar to ones in western countries must be provided by the government since there are no enough jobs for all the citizens and most people live in poverty. In addition, there are enough resources to generate money for this service such as oil. The government must provide free medical care for its citizens because ordinary citizens cannot afford these services. Oil revenues must be shared and each family should be given cash assistances. Foods need to be subsidized and government can also build subsidized housings in every city or town for those who cannot afford and perhaps let citizens live there for free until they have incomes to pay their share.

Ninth: The South Sudan government must guarantee Civil Society a freedom to exercise its right in order to have true democracy in South Sudan and there must be free and fair elections in the country.

REFERENCES

Andzejewski, J. (2009, April 3). *Social justice, peace, and environmental education: Transformative standards (1ʷed.). New York and London: Routledge; Taylor & Francis Group.*

Aras, D. (2011). *Sudan's ticking time bombs. Middle East Quarterly, 18(4), 79-84.*

Arnold, M. (2007). *The South Sudan defense force: Patriots, collaborators or spoilers? Journal of Modern African Studies, 45(4), 489-516.*

Asuni, J. B. (2009). *The United States Institute of Peace (p. 3). Retrieved from www.usip.org/.*

Bond, P. (2006). *Looting Africa: The economics of exploitation. Scottville, South Africa: University of KwaZulu–Natal Press.*

Bosshard, P. (2007, May). *China's role in financing African infrastructure: Policy director. International Rivers Network.*

Bixler, M. (2006). *The lost boys of Sudan: An American story of the refugee experience (Pbk. ed.). Athens: University of Georgia Press.*

Callinicos, A. (1999). *Social theory: A historical introduction. Washington Square, NY: New York University Press.*

Carmin, J., & Agyeman, J. (2011). *Environmental inequalities beyond borders: Local perspectives on global justices. Massachusetts: The MIT Press.*

Civil war-the SPLM/A Revolution and struggle for the New Sudan. (2007). *Retrieved from http://www.splmtoday.com.*

Collier P., & Elliot, V. L. (2003). *Breaking the conflict tape: Civil War and development policy. Washington, DC: Co-publication of the World Bank and Oxford Press.*

Crone, A. J. (2007). *How do we solve our social problem? Thousand Oaks California: Pine Forges Press.*

Dagne, T. (2010, May, 28). *Sudan: The crisis in Darfur and States of the North-South peace Agreement: specialists in Africa Affair.*

Daly, M. W., &Sikainga, A. A. (Eds.).(1993). *Civil War in the Sudan. London: British Academic Press.*

De Maio, J. (2008). *Darfur into Chad: Managing the Tran nationalization of Civil War. Conference Papers—International Studies Association, 1.* Retrieved from Academic Search Premier Database.

De Waal, A. (2007). *The wars of Sudan. Nation, 284(11), 16-20.* Retrieved from Academic Search Premier Database.

Deng, F. M. (1995). *War of visions.* Washington, DC: Brookings Institute.

Deng, F. M. (2001). *Sudan—Civil War and genocide. Middle East Quarterly, 8(1),* 13.

Deng, F. M. (2001, Winter). *Middle East Quarterly, 8(1),* 13, 9p.

Deng, L. (2005). *The Sudan Comprehensive Peace Agreement: Will it be sustained? Civil Wars, 7(3),* 244-257.

Derber, C. 2011). *The wilding of America.* New York: Worth Publishers.

Dornstein, K. (Producer). (2009) *Ghana: Digital dumping. [Frontline/PBS].* WGH: Educational Foundation.

Douglas, J. (2003). *The root causes of Sudan's civil wars.* Bloomington, IN: Indiana University Press.

Edgar, O. (2000). *Sudan, civil war and terrorism.* England, UK: McMillan Press.

Fanon, F. (2004). *The wrenched of the earth.* New York, NY: Grove Press.

Fegley, R. (2009). *Title local needs and agency conflict: A case study of KajoKeji County in South Sudan. The Online Journal of African Studies, 11(1).*

Freeman, J., &Vermeule, A.(2007, August). *Massachusetts v. EPA: From politics to expertise.* Available at SSRN: http://ssrn.com/abstract=1008906.

Harir, S., & T. Tvedt. (Eds.). (1994). *Short-cut to decay: The case of Sudan.* Uppsala: NordiskaAfrikainstitutet.

Harman, D. (2001, September 6). *In Sudan, soldiers become children again. (Cover story). Christian Science Monitor,* p. 1.

Haynes, J. (2007). *Religion, ethnicity and civil war in Africa: The cases of Uganda and Sudan. Round Table, 96(390),* 305-317.

Healey, M. C. (2009). *Resilient salmon, resilient fisheries for British Columbia, Canada. Ecology and Society, 14(1),* 2.

Huff, M., & Philips, P. (2011). *Censored 2011.* New York: Seven Stories Press.

Human Rights Watch/Africa. (1994). *Civilian devastations: Abuses by all parties in the war in Southern Sudan.* New York: Human Rights Watch.

Johnson, D. (1994). *Nuer prophets.* Oxford: Clarendon Press.

Johnson, D. (1998). *The Sudan People's Liberation Army and the problem of factionalism' in C. Clapham ed., African guerillas. Oxford: James Currey, 53-72*

Johnson, D. H. (2003). *The root causes of Sudan's civil wars. Blooming, IN: University Press.*

Jok, J. M., & Hutchinson, S. E. (1999). *Sudan's prolonged civil war and the militarization of Nuer and Dinka ethnic identities. African Studies Review, 42(2), 125-45.*

Khalid, M. (2003). *War and peace in Sudan: A tale of two countries. Kegan Paul, Intl.*

Klein, N. (2007). *The shock doctrine: The rise of disaster capitalism. New York, NY: Henry Holt and Company.*

Le Billon, P. (2010). *Oil and armed conflicts in Africa. African Geographical Review, 29(1), 63-90.*

Malual, J. D. (2009). *Sustainable livelihoods analysis of post-conflict in rural development in South Sudan. Master Abstract International, 47(01), 0184. Retrieved from Academic Search Premier Database.*

McFarland, S. (2008). *The victimization of the Nuba women of the Sudan. Journal of Third World Studies, 25(2), 21-37. Retrieved from Academic Search Premier Database.*

Middle East Quarterly. (2011, Fall), 18(4), 79-84, 6p.

Mohamed Salih, M. A., &Harir, S. (1994). *Tribal militias: The genesis of national disintegration. In S. Harir& T. Tvedt, Short-cut to decay (pp. 186-203).*

Nasong'O, S. W., &Murunga, G. R. (2005) *Lack of consensus on constitutive fundamentals: Roots of the Sudanese Civil War and prospects for settlement. African & Asian Studies, 4(1/2), 51-82. Retrieved from Academic Search Premier Database.*

New African.2012, March & April), 1, 47. Web version.

Nyaba, P. A. (1997). *The politics of Liberation in South Sudan: An insider's view. Kampala: Fountain Publishers.*

Oil wars—Sudan. (2002). Retrieved fromhttp://www.youtube.com/watch=rgZ1aal478s.

Pellow, M. D. (2007). *Resisting the global toxics: Transnational movements for environmental justice. Cambridge, MA: The MIT Press.*

Perkins, J. (2005). *Confession of economic hit man. London, UK: Ebury Press.*

Perry, A., & Boswell, A. (2011). Can Sudan split without falling apart? *Time,177(1), 42-49.*

Petras, J. (2005) Empire with imperialisms. *Nova, Scotia, Canada: Fern Wood Publishing.*

Petterson, D. (1999). *Inside Sudan: Political Islam, conflict and catastrophe.* Boulder, CO: West view Press.

Ranger, T. (1983). *The invention of tradition in colonial Africa. In E. Hobsbawm& T. Ranger (Eds.). The invention of tradition. Cambridge:* Canto.

Reyna, S. P. (2010). *The disasters of war in Darfur, 1950-2004. Third World Quarterly, 31(8), 1297-1320. doi:10.1080/01436597.2010.541083.*

Rwonmire, A. (2001). *Social problems in Africa. West Port, CT: Praeger* Publishers.

Sachs. J. (2005). *The end of poverty. New York: The Penguin Press.*

Schraeder, P. J. (1993). *U.S. intervention in the Horn of Africa amidst the end of the Cold War.(Cover story). Africa Today, 40(2), 7.*

Sharon Elaine Hutchinson. (2000, June). *Anthropology Today, 16(3), 6-13. Stable URL: http://www.jstor.org/stable/2678167.*

Sharon E. Hutchinson. (2001). *The Journal of Modern African Studies, 39, 307-331. Cambridge University Press. DOI: 10.1017/S0022278X01003639 (About DOI) Published online: 26 June 2001.*

Steve, C., &Boop, D. (2010, January). *Civil War and life chances: A multinational study. International Sociology, 25(1), 75-97. Retrieved from Academic Search Premier Database.*

Stewart, F., & Fitzgerald, V. (Eds.). (2001). *War and underdevelopment: The economic and social consequences of conflict. Oxford: Oxford University Press.*

Stone, R. (Director). (2010). *[PSB Video]. American Experience Film.*

Sudan. (2003, November 15). *African Times. Retrieved from http://search. proquest.com.*

Suleiman, M. (1997). *Civil War in Sudan: The impact of ecological degradation. Contributions in Black Studies, 15.*

The longest war—Sudan. (2004). *Retrieved from http://www.youtube.com/ watch?v=gB8n44fX-U0&feature=channel.*

The Nation. 2007, March 19). *Web version.*

The New York Times. (1977, December 19), p. 31.

Thomas, E., Dr. (1999-2010). *Against the gathering storm: Securing Sudan's comprehensive peace agreement.*

Turton, D. (1997). *War and ethnicity: Global connections and violation in northeast Africa and former Yugoslavia. Oxford Dev Stud.*

Ulansey, D. (Director) & Van Burg, C. (Producer).(2009). *Call of life. [Documentary]. Facing the Mass Extinction. United State: Species Alliance Production.*

Witthoft, B. (2007). *Out of Africa: Misrepresenting Sudan's 'Lost Boys'. Forced Migration Review, (27), 65-66.*

Wood, E. (2002). *The origin of capitalism. London, UK: Vero Press.*

Zambakari, C. (2012). *The two Sudans: Elusive peace? New African, (516), 46-48.*

http://www.usip.org/publications/blood-oil-in-the-niger-delta

http://www.sudanactionnow.com

http://www.enoughproject.org/about

http://www.genocideintervention.net/

http://www.sudantribune.com/

http://www.southsudan.net/

http://www.splamilitary.net/

https://www.cia.gov/library/publications/the-world-factbook/geos/od.html/

ABOUT THE AUTHOR

Nhial Ruach is a South Sudanese American who came to the United States in 1994 through the United Nations Refugees Resettlement Program. After he was displaced by the civil war in his native country (South Sudan) in 1987, he trekked to Ethiopia where he lived as a refugee. He spent a total of eight years in Refugees camps both in Ethiopia and in Kenya.

In 2002, he enlisted in the United States Army where he proudly served for twelve years. He had been deployed to Iraq for 16 months during Operation Iraqi Freedom, and he is now a veteran of the United Stated military. For the desire of education and pursuit of this dream, he left his parents behind in his native country at the age of twelve to pursue his education in Refugee camps in Ethiopia since civil war in his native country disrupted his education. After many years of hardship in refugee camps and additional years of struggle in the United States, he eventually achieved his Bachelor's of Sciences in Electronic Engineering and a Masters' of science in Social Responsibility (Peace, Social Justice, and Environmental Justice) in the United States.

Printed in the United States
By Bookmasters